GOD HAS SEEN US

GOD HAS SEEN US

DIOSPI SUYANA
A Story Shared Around the World

Klaus-Dieter John

Translated by Janet Yachoua and Jennifer Baldwin

MONARCH
BOOKS

Published by
Lion Hudson Limited
Wilkinson House, Jordan Hill Business Park
Banbury Road, Oxford OX2 8DR, England
www.lionhudson.com

ISBN 978 0 85721 944 2

e-ISBN 978 0 85721 945 9

First English language edition 2019

Original edition published in German as *Gott hat uns gesehen* by Brunnen Verlag GmbH. Copyright: Klaus-Dieter John, "Gott hat uns gesehen", © Brunnen Verlag GmbH, Gießen 2015, www.brunnen-verlag.de

Acknowledgments

Cover design based on the German edition by Brunnen Verlag GmbH.

Scripture quotations marked (NET) are from the NET Bible® copyright ©1996-2006 by Biblical Studies Press, L.L.C. http://bible.org All rights reserved.

Scripture quotations marked (NIV) taken from the Holy Bible, New International Version Anglicised. Copyright 1979, 1984, 2011 Biblica, formerly International Bible Society. Used by permission of Hodder & Stoughton Ltd, an Hachette UK company. All rights reserved. "NIV" is a registered trademark of Biblica. UK trademark number 1448790.

Scripture quotations marked (ESV) are from The Holy Bible, English Standard Version® (ESV®) copyright © 2001 by Crossway, a publishing ministry of Good News Publishers. All rights reserved.

A catalogue record for this book is available from the British Library

Printed and bound in the UK, July 2019, LH26

Dear Natalie, Dominik and Florian,
may our family's story remind you that
God has seen all five of us. And not just us –
but the whole world.

Contents

Acknowledgments

My wife and I wish to thank all our volunteers and members of staff, and friends of our work worldwide, for their faithfulness to us, when we are anything but perfect.

In the New Testament, Paul writes: "[God] is able to do immeasurably more than all we ask or imagine, according to his power that is at work within us" (Ephesians 3:20, NIV). This proclamation has been proven repeatedly throughout the fascinating story of Diospi Suyana. We thank God for His faithfulness.

Johann Sebastian Bach wrote the initials "SDG" at the end of all his compositions. SDG stands for *Soli Deo Gloria*, which means "to God alone be the glory". We thank God for His presence in our lives and His promises for our future. As for us, we have set our hope on heaven, where we will one day live with God forever.

And we pray with Christians of all denominations: Maranatha, come Lord Jesus, come soon!

Foreword

When faced with a success, some people credit hard work, and others chalk it up to coincidence and luck.

But the truth is, when we – ordinary people – acknowledge our limitations and hand our lives over to God for His purpose, He can and will do great things.

Our almighty God is not some distant creator of the universe; nor is He a vending machine that chucks out the desired answers to all our prayers. He does not promise riches, power, health or well-being. Instead, He promises Himself – His power at work in us, His Spirit guiding us. We can all know Him as our helper and saviour. Sometimes His presence is so powerful we break out in goosebumps. Other times, He is as gentle as a whisper. He brings joy that can cause us to laugh out loud. But above all, His faithfulness is unchanging. We can trust Him completely, putting our lives in His hands, knowing that He loves us. It is not about our personal efforts, but about recognizing that He is the Lord.

The tales shared in this book are an invitation to risk experiencing God yourself. In sharing them, we aim to testify to God's greatness and goodness. This is the breath-taking continuation of the story God has written – and keeps writing – with and for the people of Diospi Suyana.

Dr Klaus-Dieter John is a man who desired to see and experience for himself that God is not the product of human imagination. He considers it a privilege to work alongside God, showing His love in action all over the world. And he is my husband. Perhaps as such, I am one of his fiercest critics, but in this I must praise him. He relates the events exactly as they occurred, demonstrating clearly how God sees and cares for all of us. This is the foundation for God's work among the Quechua people in the Peruvian Andes.

Diospi Suyana was an idea conceived in love, to show a people they are not forgotten.

Dr Martina John

1

The Catastrophe

There hadn't been a rainy season like it in human memory. Just after Christmas of 2009, the sky turned an ominous grey. Weeks passed, one thunderstorm giving way to the next. The continuous rumbling of thunder and intense flashes of lightning contributed to the threatening ambience, but the rain itself was the real danger. Rivers surged and overflowed their banks. Entire mountain slopes were compromised in the deluge; massive landslides buried roads and train tracks daily and with little warning. The inhabitants of the southern Andes were desperate for the dry season to begin.

I cast a worried glance at my watch. Nurse Michael Mörl and his family were returning to Curahuasi that evening after spending some time in Germany. The road they would need to travel was flooded near the Apurímac and nearly impassable, save for a single lane in some locations. Road workers toiled around the clock with their heavy equipment to facilitate passage through the mud where it had completely blocked the Pan-American Highway.

Damaris Hassfeld, another nurse, had kindly offered to drive to Cusco airport to pick up the Mörls. The journey through the mountains on a night such as this would be extremely perilous. I felt a disturbing sense of foreboding as I parked at the Mörls' home and peered through the misty windscreen into the darkness.

At the same time, Michael Mörl was peering with great effort and concentration through the windscreen of another vehicle. His wife Elisabeth, his children and Damaris Hassfeld walked ahead of the minivan, through the torrential rain. Getting wet was of no consequence compared to the danger of being in the vehicle at this point. The river had risen to the level of the road, and chunks of asphalt were breaking off and washing away at an alarming rate. The noise was deafening – and terrifying.

Elisabeth drew her children, Nicodemus and Leonore, close to her. As cold, wet, and exhausted as they were, she reassured them that they were nearly home.

As Elisabeth and the children reached a wider stretch of road, they lost sight of Michael behind them. They anxiously waited for him, realizing how careful he would need to be in order to safely navigate the narrow bit of road that remained.

Michael waited until he could see the others were on solid ground. Then he took a deep breath and hit the accelerator, literally flying past the dark floodwaters on his left and the steep drop on his right. As he landed safely, he was unaware that in two hours' time, that section of road would be completely obliterated by the raging waters.

The Mörl family and Damaris Hassfeld finally arrived home at 9:30 p.m. – exhausted, grateful, and very unlikely to forget the events of the last few hours. With great relief I bade them a good night and set out for my own home to get some sleep. Little did I know that the adventures of the evening were far from over.

I was suddenly awakened by what seemed to be the sound of pebbles hitting my bedroom window. Martina was on night duty at the hospital. I jumped up and grabbed my shoes. When I drew the curtain from the window, I could see Dr David Brady, our urologist, standing next to his pick-up truck with the engine still running. He waved his arms frantically, calling me to come to the hospital immediately. A bus had overturned on the road near Sayhuite. The team was expecting the worst.

That was all I needed to hear, and I scrambled to get myself together to leave. I knew from the Mörls' experience that the road to Cusco was now impassable. But this bus had been coming from the other direction. Perhaps the driver had been overcome by fatigue, or perhaps the brakes had failed, or perhaps rocks and debris in the road had caused the bus to overturn. Regardless of the reason for the accident, Diospi Suyana was the closest hospital and we all now had a task requiring our best team effort.

It was 3 a.m. when David and I hurried through the rear entrance to the hospital. My wife was busy in the emergency room with four victims who had already arrived via taxi. More were on their way. David grabbed gloves and began to help Martina. I ran back to the car and headed into town to gather as many staff as possible. A catastrophe of this magnitude was going to require all of us.

I sped from house to house, rousing nurses, surgeons, and lab technicians. Once awake, staff used their mobile phones to spread the alarm. Within minutes, all key hospital personnel had been notified.

I am certain that Michael Mörl did not expect to be seeing me again that night; nor did he expect to be called in to work so soon and under such dire circumstances. Despite jetlag, the experienced intensive-care nurse immediately answered our urgent call.

As we ran through the hospital corridors together, we saw patients on beds and stretchers everywhere, covered in blood, and shaking like leaves from the shock of the accident and their wet clothing. Tina, David, and Dr Oliver Engelhard were in the process of triaging victims as they arrived.

"Klaus, you need to get to the operating room immediately!" barked Oliver. "This one has acute abdomen trauma and is in shock!"

I swallowed hard. During my recent time spent away, sharing the story and obtaining funding for Diospi Suyana, such surgeries had normally been conducted by Dr Daniel Zeyse – who was now on holiday with his family.

We rushed to the operating theatre with four nurses and an anaesthesiologist in tow. Dr Dripps, a Harvard University professor volunteering with Diospi Suyana for four months, quickly administered the anaesthetic. I offered a brief "arrow prayer" for blessing, then sliced through the man's abdomen to find his liver torn and spewing blood into the abdominal cavity. I stopped the bleeding with compresses, then sutures. A repeat operation would be necessary in forty-eight hours.

The number of casualties rose with every vehicle that arrived at the hospital. Diospi Suyana staff fought for each and every victim, all night long. Even those not trained in medicine, such as computer specialist Benjamin Azuero, helped in whatever way they could. In the radiology department, paediatrician Dr Frick and Ester Litzau quickly pushed patients through the CT machine. Afterwards, it was discovered that these courageous and tireless staff completed a total of 148 X-rays and CT scans in those fateful hours of 25 January.

Doctors from nearby medical clinics joined our ranks, quickly suturing wounds of all sizes as if on an assembly

GOD HAS SEEN US

line. It was a very long night, but by 6 a.m. we could start to breathe once again. Fifty-three of the accident victims were expected to survive.

One woman was dead upon arrival at the hospital, and all efforts to resuscitate her proved futile. Martina and I accompanied her distraught daughter to the morgue – the least we could do in the face of her tragic death.

At 8 a.m. we had no choice but to send home the outpatient visitors queuing outside the hospital doors. Even though some of them had travelled a great distance for our help, not one complained. It was as though they had an understanding of what had transpired the night before and were responding with both empathy and solidarity.

Christian Contreras was a medical student from Lima, completing an internship at Diospi Suyana at the time of this crisis. Not only was he an eye witness, he was also able to capture photos on his phone as the events of that night unfolded. Even years later, he shares his pictures and stories at every suitable opportunity, bearing personal testimony to an incredible experience.

2

The Aftermath

That afternoon, most staff went home and dropped into bed, completely exhausted, which was to be expected after having been up all night and on their feet for twelve hours, desperately rushing around the hospital to save the victims of that horrific accident.

Meanwhile, all the test and scan results were back, indicating that four patients urgently required transfer to Cusco. My patient with the torn liver would need his second surgery, and it was necessary for that surgery to be completed at a hospital with a sufficient supply of blood in case profuse bleeding resumed. Another patient was completely unrecognizable owing to extensive swelling and broken bones in her face. She needed the expertise of a plastic surgeon. Still another patient, a woman called Benita Sutta, was essentially paralysed with a suspected fracture of her top vertebra. Finally, there was a young man with suspected leukaemia. The CT had revealed a large haematoma in his spleen. If this were to rupture, the man would bleed to death within minutes.

So four patients needed to get to Cusco as soon as possible – but how? Many stretches of the main road between Curahuasi and Cusco had been destroyed by the flooding, and there was no alternative route. Air travel appeared to be our only option.

GOD HAS SEEN US

From midday, just hours after the accident, I began continuously phoning the Ministry of Health in Lima, in the hope of securing some helicopter support. I also called the office of the First Lady, Pilar Nores de García. In 2006, the wife of the Peruvian Head of State had promised her support to Diospi Suyana for whenever we had need – and now the time had come. In other parts of the world, arranging a thirty-five-minute helicopter ride for four patients might seem like a fairly routine task. But in the Peruvian Andes, the situation was very different. There simply were no helicopters at all in Cusco, and no organized regional rescue network in place. If a helicopter were to become available somewhere, it would not be deployed to assist until the matter of payment had been settled.

To further complicate matters, our four patients were not the only ones requiring air rescue. A gigantic landslide had just displaced sections of the Peru Rail lines between Machu Picchu and Cusco. More than 2,000 tourists were stuck in local towns and villages, having spent the night in make-shift tents instead of the luxury hotels they had booked.

Machu Picchu is one of the "new" Seven Wonders of the World, attracting more than 2 million visitors annually from all over the globe. Its popularity stems from its combination of Inca heritage, breath-taking scenery, impressive ruins, and – for those of the New Age persuasion – its reported mystical energies. When there is trouble at Machu Picchu, the world pays attention.

The plight of the stranded tourists made headlines not only in Peru, but in Europe and the USA as well. The government of Peru had to take immediate, visible action. Out of this political necessity, the Peruvian military began to airlift the tourists out of their predicament. The reality is that tourists are not just people, they are also a source of much-needed income – a simple fact that bears great significance.

As the crow flies, Machu Picchu is only about thirty miles from Curahuasi, on the other side of the mountain range. From my window, I could see the helicopters on the horizon and even hear the whirring of their propellers. Wistfully, I looked over to the snow-capped mountains. The government of Peru was sparing no expense or effort for the tourists. The Air Force pilots shuttled out healthy tourists while our four seriously injured patients languished. It was time to bring our plight to the attention of the media.

"Michael!" I called out to our intensive-care nurse. "Could you possibly film our patients in the intensive care unit? I would like to email the video clips to TV Channel 2. People need to see what is going on here!"

"Yes, I can manage that," replied Michael, as he went off in search of his camera. Between the jetlag, lack of sleep, and stressful events, he was clearly exhausted – but as always, he was willing to do whatever needed to be done. Before long, he had sent me several short video segments, which I then forwarded to Renato Canales. Renato Canales was not just "anybody" – he was the executive director of *90 Segundos*, Peru's leading news programme. He had known us since 2006 and had already broadcast five extensive reports on our hospital. Over the years, he had become extremely supportive of Diospi Suyana, and he promised to help us in our current plight.

That very evening, Michael's videos were televised nationally. The basic message was impossible to miss: in Curahuasi, four seriously injured patients were being denied access to life-saving treatment in Cusco while the military prioritized the transport of healthy tourists from Machu Picchu – purely for reasons of publicity and propaganda!

I also continued to vent my personal dissatisfaction with the situation until late that night, sending long emails to the Minister of Health, Oscar Ugarte, and the First Lady, attaching fourteen rather graphic photos, as pictures are indeed often worth a thousand words.

The next day, 26 January, things finally started to move. I had previously started negotiations with the South American Rescue Association Peru (SARA), a fairly new organization that, among other things, hired helicopters from private Peruvian companies and arranged emergency flights as needed – and as could be paid for. The service was usually reimbursed at a good profit by foreign insurance companies. My contact at SARA was the vice-president, Bernhard Farnheim, a German from the southern state of Baden-Württemberg.

The First Lady responded to my emails, informing me that she had contacted both the Prime Minister and the head of the Air Force on our behalf. She assured me that they would soon come to our aid. However, I received no response from the military, even after twenty-four hours.

The Ministry of Health was a different matter, and progress was becoming evident. Dr Estela Flores contacted me by phone to share the good news that two SARA flights had been arranged with costs covered, securing the evacuation of our four patients. I sighed deeply with relief and rubbed my weary eyes. "Finally!" I mumbled to myself. "That took some doing!" Now we just needed to wait for the helicopters to arrive.

Even with Dr Flores' verbal assurance, I knew I needed to actively pursue the helicopter assistance until it had in fact arrived. I called the SARA office in Cusco every half an hour with the same questions: "Where are you? How much longer will you be?"

The responses were frustrating, vague, and occasionally contradictory. One employee told me that the helicopter was approaching our location. Another told us it hadn't even taken off yet from Quillabamba, and therefore would not be arriving for several hours. I lost my temper several times, sensing that some were more concerned with making money than with the well-being of our patients.

By 3:30 p.m. I had almost given up hope of the helicopter arriving that day. Then I heard a gentle whirring in the air, which grew into a loud roar. The long-awaited SARA helicopter had arrived! It landed on the most beautiful helipad in the Apurímac, which of course was located at our hospital. Without further delay, we moved my patient with the ruptured liver and the woman with the fractured vertebra on board. Nurse Silvia Vargas and I boarded as the medical supervision for the flight. I took my small suitcase and laptop bag, as I would be continuing on to Lima in order to make a previously scheduled connecting flight to the USA. In less than twenty-four hours, I had an appointment with Vitor Rocha, a GE Healthcare representative, who was considering my request for the company to donate an image converter, an indispensable aid during surgery to repair bone fractures. The machine was extremely expensive and I had been asked to make my formal request and presentation in person – in Miami.

The helicopter door banged shut loudly, the engine revved, and the propeller spun faster and faster until it was only a blur. We took off and headed towards Cusco as fifty members of the hospital staff watched our departure. I had my camera and was suddenly inspired to take some aerial shots of the hospital. As a child, I had once been captivated by a picture of the Dalai Lama's palace. But the sight of Diospi Suyana hospital, fixed on this mountain slope, was absolutely mesmerizing. My wife and I had invested so much for so long to bring this hospital from dream to life. I looked on, full of gratitude, as the hospital grounds grew smaller and smaller, then finally disappeared from sight.

We touched down safely at Cusco airport just thirty-four minutes later. A private ambulance from EsSalud would be arriving to pick up our patients shortly. I glanced towards the airport terminal nervously. There was my plane. It was the last flight of the day to Lima. I had my ticket in the inside pocket of my jacket. I knew that in nine minutes the doors would close and the plane would begin its taxi to the runway.

My thoughts began to race. If I proceeded immediately to the terminal via the entrance, and properly went through security and identification checks, it would take at least a quarter of an hour, if I was even permitted through at this late stage. I would miss my flight! No, there was only one option if I was going to make it onto that plane.

I called out a hasty *"Hasta luego!"* to the helicopter crew, grabbed my bags, and bounded like a maniac across the tarmac towards the plane. The jetway had steps descending to the ground. I leapt up them, squeezed through the side door, and found myself in front of two speechless flight attendants.

The two ladies clearly struggled to maintain composure. They had never experienced someone bypassing security and crashing through the side door of the jetway before. For all they knew, I could be dangerous.

"No, you are too late! We are due for take-off and your luggage has not been screened!"

I frowned. To be so close – it just had to work, somehow. I quickly pulled out a hospital brochure from my bag and indicated the endorsement from the First Lady. "Pilar Nores is a supporter of our hospital in Curahuasi. You have to help me!"

It was sufficient. "OK, come quickly!" one of them called. "We will get your bags scanned."

The pretty flight attendant turned out to be a mean sprinter. Two minutes later, the aircraft doors were closed and I was settled in my seat, on my way to Lima and then Miami.

Back at Diospi Suyana, the helicopter returned at about 5:30 p.m. to pick up the two remaining critical patients. They were able to reach Cusco airport before darkness fell. That night, I wrote an update for the Diospi Suyana website, closing with the words, "It is good to have such an exciting life, but does it really have to be *so* exciting?"

My flight to Miami went smoothly, and by 9 a.m. I was standing sharp and ready in front of the GE Healthcare building. The towering palm trees and bright blue sky almost made it feel like a holiday, but I was there on an important mission.

Mr Vitor Rocha, a native of Brazil, patiently attended my presentation. He was courteous but somewhat aloof. When I was finished, he announced that he was not the right person to contact, and others would need to make the decision regarding the possible donation of the image converter. I looked at him in utter disbelief. I had just flown more than 3,000 miles at great expense and effort for this meeting. I was beginning to be concerned that the stress of the last two days had been for nothing.

Many of our friends are well versed in the high points of the Diospi Suyana story. At times we seem to zip from one brilliant success to another – a large financial donation here, a personal audience with a prominent person there, daunting obstacles surmounted effortlessly, and so on. The "thorns" and frustrating situations are often quickly forgotten. I personally think these challenges have deep meaning and should not be overlooked. They show how difficult it really has been to start and run our hospital. They drive us to pray more intensely for God's intervention. When the answers do come, they are often nothing short of miraculous.

That afternoon, I was back on an aeroplane. Before returning to Peru, I was flying to Barcelona at the invitation of Equip Mèdic de Salut Integral (EMSI), a humanitarian aid society that regularly sends medical teams to Africa. So now I had the opportunity to share the story of Diospi Suyana with thirty Christian doctors and nurses. Naturally, I saw these Spanish-speaking volunteers as potential short- and long-term missionaries for our hospital in Peru.

We met at the Protestant Hospital in Barcelona and clicked immediately. Several doctors communicated great interest in our work. One of them, Dr Alfonso Miranda from Cadiz, wanted to do much more than talk. Several months later, the experienced anaesthesiologist joined our team at Curahuasi during his summer holidays. His reward was twofold. While he was with us, Spain won the World Cup! We all still have Alfonso's cheer ringing in our ears as Spain scored the winning goal. His second reward was considerably greater: he fell in love with our chief theatre nurse, Ulrike

Beck. They married a year later and currently reside happily in his home town in the south of Spain.

During that eventful week in January, we had a Swiss couple volunteering with us short term. Peter Wettstein was helping out in the workshop, and his wife Karin was in anaesthesiology. On 1 February they had planned a trip into Cusco. Normally, this would have been a two-and-a-half-hour trip, but with all the destruction from the recent flooding, travellers now had to vacate their vehicles at two different points along the road and climb along the mountain slope until they could obtain transportation to the next valley. As the Wettsteins were experienced alpine hikers, they were not particularly bothered by this inconvenience.

The Wettsteins joined a group of travellers halfway between the Apurímac River crossing and the little town of Limatambo. They had already reached an elevation of 150 metres (500 feet). The path over the mountain slope was narrow and not for the unsteady. No one knows how or why it happened; if it was a lapse in concentration or faulty footwear. Karin suddenly lost her footing, tumbled more than 100 metres down the side of the mountain and plummeted the last 30 metres in free fall. Peter looked on in horror as his wife disappeared over the precipice.

When Peter finally found Karin, she was lying flat on her back on the red corrugated roof of a Catholic chapel. The flexible roof tiles had functioned as a fireman's blanket, the suspension breaking her fall and saving her life. The chapel was the only building within two and a half miles that was located along the road. The probability of her landing on the roof of that lone building was slim to none.

GOD HAS SEEN US

Karin was alive but seriously injured. She sustained fractures to the lumbar region of her spine, one of her hips, her pelvis, and her heel bone. With the whole valley essentially turned into a river bed at that one point, there was only one option for safely evacuating Karin.

Caring roadworkers placed her into the scoop of one of their bulldozers and transported her two miles up the Rio Blanco. The pain she experienced during this rough ride would have been excruciating. An ambulance was waiting to take Karin from Limatambo to Cusco. From there she was flown to a private clinic in Lima. Her saga of suffering continued, as her first operation in Peru resulted in a serious infection. More operations were required back home in Switzerland, then a month of rehab. It took an entire year for Karin to recover fully; a year full of discouraging setbacks and endless tests of her patience.

Three hours after Karin's fall, I was heading home from my trip to Spain, and I passed the site from the opposite side. I had no idea what had happened at this point, but I did know that three hikers had fallen to their death on this slope in the last several days. Karin had very nearly been the fourth. Not being comfortable with heights myself, I declined to cross the slope, and instead went with a guide through the mountains on the other side of the river. During the ninety-minute trek, I took photos of the valley beneath me. Without knowing about Karin's accident, I unwittingly documented the approximate trajectory of her fall. Looking at the photos, it is nearly impossible to believe that someone could have survived such a drop.

Karin and Peter Wettstein, their friends, and the staff at Diospi Suyana all thank God for protecting her during this terrible time. One might argue that God could have easily prevented the accident, and question why He allowed it to even occur.

The question of human suffering continually occupies our thoughts at Diospi Suyana, whether we are conscious of it or not. Impersonal case files quickly develop true humanity as we look into the eyes of a patient and listen to his or her story and expressions of pain. When we spend long nights striving in vain to wrest a young child or an expectant mother from death, our heartbreak is just as real as our exhaustion. And the cry of our hearts is, "Why, God?"

Anyone who claims to know the answer to this question has clearly never worked in intensive care. The endless grief and pain that accompanies us every day indicates one thing: the definitive response to suffering cannot be found in modern medicine, but only in faith. When God carries us through the valley of death, we find security we can hold on to. When He waits for us in love on the other side, we find comfort and peace – so much more than morphine or Valium can ever provide.

God's faithfulness is the reason why my wife and I founded the mission hospital. Every morning we hold a worship service in the hospital chapel with 200 patients and staff. We remind one another of God's love for us and read in our Bibles about God's unchanging promises. These thirty minutes help us to better understand, even if just a little bit, that every hope we have is in the grace of God alone.

3

Smear Campaign

Three months had passed since the horrific bus crash, and life at Diospi Suyana was returning to normal. At the end of April 2010, I was surprised by a phone call from Alexander Chavarry, the managing director of SARA Peru. He informed me that the Ministry of Health had unfortunately not completely covered the helicopter rescue costs, and he requested that I use my influence in Lima to expedite a resolution.

I couldn't quite figure out what to make of this phone call, but something definitely seemed "off". I chose my words carefully as I informed Mr Chavarry that Diospi Suyana had not been party to the financial details of the helicopter service. The Ministry of Health and SARA had communicated directly and reportedly reached a mutual agreement on the matter.

On Saturday 1 May, I opened my emails to find an angry message from Bernhard Farnheim, the vice-president of SARA Peru. He expressed clear annoyance that I had not intervened with the Ministry of Health on behalf of the financial interests of his company.

Although I have been aware of the vengeance that can be publicly displayed during an argument here in Peru, I was not prepared for the personal insults that followed in Mr Farnheim's email. He accused me of having delusions of grandeur and of having lost touch with reality. He further claimed that what I credited on our website as "God's intervention" was evidence of a personality disorder.

The email was egregious. I read through the short text a second, then a third time. My gaze shifted to the designated message recipients – and I froze. Bernhard Farnheim had sent this vitriol to a never-ending list of people. I was horrified to see that he had copied staff members at the German embassy, the ambassador himself, a member of the German parliament in Berlin, a minister of the Hessian state government, and a whole series of NGOs in various countries, including companies such as Volkswagen and others with whom I had positive working relationships.

I was so upset as I printed off the list. Mr Farnheim had trashed my name and reputation in an email sent to 400 people. Perhaps the word "panic" most accurately describes what I felt at that moment. I called Tina into my office and pointed at the computer screen. My wife skimmed the email, shaking her head in horror and disbelief. We both just stood there. Numb.

How should we respond to such a personal assault on our mission and character? Tina and I shared a word in prayer, then I contacted our civil engineer, Udo Klemenz, and told him what had just happened. In his many years of experience leading construction teams all over the world, he had dealt with aggressive confrontation on more than one occasion; perhaps he would have some advice for us.

An hour later, we had a battle plan. We would send a separate message to each recipient of the original missive, directly addressing Mr Farnheim's personal insults and clarifying the facts, one by one.

The feeling you get when the ground seems to quake beneath your feet and falling seems imminent, as if you are trying to balance on a mountain of jelly – that was exactly how I felt. Discouraged. Dejected. The email from the vice-president of SARA weighed on me heavily all day, invaded my sleep, then rudely awakened me again the next morning. I calculated that, based on the cc list, as many as 800 people could have read those slanderous remarks about me. I began to feel a bit sorry for myself and questioned why God had allowed this to happen. We were serving in His name under tremendously adverse conditions in the Peruvian highlands. The Diospi Suyana hospital had proven a blessing for indigenous people all over Peru. We had fought beyond our strength for the four critically injured bus accident victims back in January. And this was our thanks? What a low blow.

I think God had a chuckle or two at my expense that weekend. Of course, He saw and cared about my pain and disappointment – but He also knew what Monday would bring. On Monday 3 May, the German TV channel ZDF broadcast a distinctly affirming report of Diospi Suyana and our work in Peru.

Those six and a half minutes were the best publicity we could ever have hoped for. My wife and I were commended as the founders of the mission hospital in front of 800,000 viewers. For every reader of Mr Farnheim's original hateful email, a thousand people had the opportunity to hear the truth and develop a positive impression of our work. Saturday's events, although only forty-eight hours in the past, now seemed like a lifetime ago. I felt comforted, strengthened, and motivated. In my mind, the SARA Peru drama was over.

The Bible tells us not to worry about the future, for each day has trouble enough of its own. I had no idea what was

GOD HAS SEEN US

going to unfold nine months later – a good thing too, as this would have cast a dark shadow on the second half of 2010.

On 20 January 2011, nearly a year to the day after the bus crash, I received a series of documents from the court in Curahuasi. My heart sank as I leafed through the pages. SARA Peru had made a claim against me as a private citizen and was suing for more than $29,000. Approximately $9,500 of this was to cover the unpaid helicopter rescue costs. The remaining $20,000 was being sought for vague "damages" incurred by SARA Peru as a result of the unpaid bill. Elements of the judicial system in Peru can be corrupt, easily influenced by bribery and "back scratching". I knew I needed to take immediate, decisive action in order to rectify the situation.

At the end of January, I flew to Lima to attempt to locate those members of the Ministry of Health who had been involved with the situation the year before. I found them all, conveniently sitting at their desks. Dr Estela Flores gave me access to detailed minutes of related discussions, which clearly indicated that the Ministry of Health in Lima, as well as the state government in Abancay (Apurímac region), had negotiated the cost of the two flights with SARA. It was well documented that they had agreed on a price of $4,500. When SARA then presented a bill for $22,000 to the Ministry, there was no upset; it was simply sent back via return post.

I then visited the state government in Abancay and obtained another document, which confirmed the information I had previously received in Lima. Of course, I also arranged for legal counsel. The Olaechea law firm in Lima has assisted us on a pro bono basis since 2008. Lawyer Efrain Caviedes of Cusco is himself an honorary member of Diospi Suyana.

Once all the facts were on the table, it was discovered that SARA Peru had received nearly $12,000 from several sources to cover the flight costs – almost three times the agreed upon amount! When neither the Ministry nor the state government responded to pressure from SARA for additional funds, they came after me as a private individual – all in efforts to get more money.

As always in such legal conflicts, there are hearings and more hearings, motions and counter-motions, and on and on. I travelled back and forth between Lima, Abancay, Cusco, and Curahuasi.

On 14 June the court courier delivered the verdict to my house. I had won the case hands down. A year and a half after the bus accident had occurred, we finally had closure.

Looking back, I reflect on what I have learned through these trials. Most importantly, I now understand that God knows the future and holds it in the palm of His hand. Things that cause us fear and distress today may evaporate into the mists of time by tomorrow.

But there is another thing I have learned: as I continue to manage the hospital, I am becoming more careful, more watchful. Once bitten, twice shy....

4

"Tear Down the Walls!"

I was just about to send the young woman at the fence away. She seemed very pushy, and that wasn't something I liked.

"What do you want here?" I demanded with my very German directness.

"I am a dentist, and I would like to see inside the hospital," she responded.

I looked her in the eye. Whether it was her pleasant smile, or the faint realization that I would not be able to get rid of her easily, I do not recall – but we began to chat.

Although we had celebrated the inauguration of Diospi Suyana on 31 August 2007, the hospital was not yet open to patients. Udo Klemenz and the construction team were completing interior details in nearly every department of the building. Floors were being tiled in the two rooms designated for dental treatment. Sooner or later, we would indeed require a dentist.

"Do you have much experience as a dentist?" I asked, once again direct.

"Oh yes, I have. I have even worked in Israel," she confirmed.

Now it was my turn to smile. A Peruvian dentist whose CV included work experience in Israel was certainly not a typical candidate! "I would be happy to show you the hospital," I replied, opening the door to let her in.

Dr Karina Herrera came, she saw, and she conquered.

There is a huge need for dental care in the Andes. It requires only one look into the open mouth of a patient to understand the extent of the problem. The old, dilapidated dentist chair we had available was made functional again through the imagination and determination of our technicians. But to conquer the demon of tooth decay and prevent the degeneration of mouths into veritable quarries, we were certainly going to need more than one chair!

On 24 July 2008, dentist Dr Dankfried Geister and his wife Dorothea flew to Peru after reading a magazine article about Diospi Suyana. Dr Geister was 60-plus years of age, with a history of multiple heart surgeries – on the surface, hardly an ideal candidate for intense labour at an altitude of 2,650 metres! But Dankfried Geister, whose name means "spirits", became a powerful and passionate force for the hospital. As soon as he and his wife heard the words "Diospi Suyana", they overflowed with enthusiasm. Even on a plane miles above the Atlantic Ocean, they shared the vision of Diospi Suyana via video with the passengers near them. Anyone who can transform a plane into a cinema in this manner is undoubtedly a fervent supporter with deep conviction.

No sooner had I shown Dankfried and Dorothea around the hospital than the wheels of his imagination began to turn.

"Klaus, you had best tear some of these walls down; then you can double the size of your dental care area!"

I didn't bat an eyelid, but in my head I thought, *Easy there, slow down! We've just got these walls* up!

Dr Geister hit the ground running. Although Dankfried obviously spoke excellent German, his Spanish skills were not quite up to par. Fortunately, at that time we had a Spanish-speaking intern from Germany who served as both translator and dental assistant. Valerio Krüger and Dr Geister made the perfect team as they restored the teeth of countless Quechua people.

I just could not let go of Dankfried's exhortation to "tear down the walls". It was obvious that a single room for dental treatment was woefully inadequate. The idea eventually emerged that walls should not be torn down – more walls should be built instead! It was time for a fully fledged Diospi Suyana dental clinic.

This proposal was readily received by Dr Geister, and he offered to draw up the plans for the dental clinic based on his own practice in Denkendorf. We found space for the clinic behind our radiology department. We firmly believed that if this project was God's will, he would provide all the resources we needed to complete it. As the German saying goes, "God pays for what he orders!"

But who would actually build the dental clinic? I reached out again to the experienced civil engineer who had overseen the construction of the hospital. Although he had left Peru in 2008, there was no doubt he was the right man for the job. On 23 June 2009 I published the breaking news on our website: "Udo Klemenz to return to Peru!" Udo and his wife Barbara had slipped into the lecture hall of the Catholic University in Gießen, where I was scheduled to speak, to let me know that they would be returning to Diospi Suyana. Construction on the dental clinic would begin that August. I could barely contain my excitement at this wonderful news, and my presentation that day was even more energetic than usual.

The contents of a parcel are usually more expensive than the actual packing materials. A dental clinic is no exception to that rule. We estimated a cost of approximately $200,000 for the clinic building. Equipping it properly would cost much, much more. We needed the blessing of some significant donations.

My thoughts turned to Claudia Dräger, the wife of the head of the Dräger Group. She had visited us at the end of August 2008 in order to personally deliver a very generous donation of seven brand new sets of equipment for our operating theatre and intensive care units. She and her team from the Lübeck-based company spent three jam-packed days in Curahuasi. Their visit naturally included the obligatory tour of the hospital, on top of the formal ceremony for the presentation of their donation, which was followed by a delicious dinner prepared by my wife and served at our home.

Claudia Dräger may not have shared our Christian faith, but she most certainly shared a deep love for the work of Diospi Suyana. As she bluntly stated during a phone call in the autumn of 2008, "Mr John, your faith stuff is totally crazy, but your hospital is great. If you ever need contacts, I would be more than happy to help you." And now we were in desperate need of those contacts, without which we would not be able to equip the dental clinic.

Ms Dräger first directed me to Salzburg, to the export director of the Sirona Group. Mr Vogel was an extremely busy and stressed-out man, as was I, but he made time to listen and considered a donation of five dental chairs. In case any dentists are becoming green with envy as they read this, please remember that the donation was not for us personally, but for the benefit of countless Quechua people.

On 3 March 2009, Ms Dräger arranged an hour-long

GOD HAS SEEN US

meeting in Washington between myself and Larry Culp, President and CEO of the Danaher Group, a massive conglomeration of forty companies. In such a position of power, his impression of Diospi Suyana was going to carry a great deal of weight. Apparently, Mr Culp liked what he heard; it was decided that the Brazilian subsidiary, Kavo, would supply five dental chairs.

I had not actually been hoping for these additional chairs, but for other specialized furniture that Kavo could provide. It was a sticky situation. The two most promising contributors to our cause had made identical offers, and only one was needed. Accepting the offer of one meant most likely offending the other and destroying any possibility of future collaboration. I poured out my heart to God in prayer, asking for His guidance in this seemingly impossible situation. His deliverance was eventually "served" on the most unlikely plate.

Several months passed after I made a visit to Kavo in São Paulo. Despite instructions from the USA head, Kavo-Brazil did not get the dental chair donation together. The delay was so long, I was able to turn down the donation without losing face. On 7 July 2009, I emailed the São Paulo office, copying Larry Culp. While grateful for their generosity, owing to time constraints I needed to accept the donation from Sirona instead.

A few days later, my phone rang while I was sitting in morning devotions at the hospital. I went outside to take the call. It was Larry Culp, apologizing that Kavo-Brazil had failed to deliver.

"Larry," I said, taking a deep breath, "maybe Kavo-Germany would be able to help us with the furniture instead. Does that seem like a workable alternative?"

The head of Danaher did not hesitate. "Yes! That is what we will do. You can have the furniture from Germany!"

Many years have passed since that brief phone call, but I have never forgotten it. Larry Culp headed up a conglomerate with an annual turnover of $20 billion. I was not a major shareholder, customer, or TV star, and yet we spoke as equals. He clearly wanted to support Diospi Suyana, whatever the cost. But why? Did he owe Claudia Dräger a favour? Probably not. Had the misery of the Quechua people touched his conscience? I don't believe so. I think the real reason is altogether different. The Bible says that we believers are ambassadors in Christ's place. We belong to the "diplomatic corps" of heaven. We serve God, the King of kings. And when we bring a piece of His kingdom to any corner of the earth, we can expect His blessings to be upon it, whether large or small.

Walking into the Kavo-Germany headquarters in Biberach on 15 September 2009, I was greeted by the manager, Henner Witte, with the words, "Mr John, you can ask for whatever you want from us – and you will get it."

In addition – and I honestly don't know whether to thank Claudia Dräger or Larry Culp for the opportunity – Stanley Bergman, CEO of Henry Schein, had given audience to my presentation four months earlier, on 12 May 2009. Henry Schein is a prominent worldwide distributor of dental supplies. The hour we spent discussing Diospi Suyana in a luxury New York hotel is one I will never forget.

Stanley Bergman is a Jew. I am a German. How many of his relatives lost their lives in the horrors of a German concentration camp? Stanley Bergman is a Jew. I am a Christian. As always, my presentation ended with the cross of Christ and the empty tomb on Easter Sunday.

And yet, the very next day, Stanley Bergman wrote to offer his assistance. His generous gift, valued at more than $200,000, would easily supply the clinic for months – though the clinic was still in the "noble idea" phase of development.

Right from the start, Udo Klemenz spurred the construction of the clinic forward as though racing against time. Our vision was for a modern dental practice with fifteen rooms, including five treatment rooms, a lab, and an X-ray room. The architects and engineers had already drawn up the plans and done their calculations. One morning, as Udo and I were reviewing them, Michael Mörl stepped into the office and made a proposal close to his heart.

"What do you think about building an optician's workshop?"

The reason behind his query was simple: his wife Elisabeth was a qualified optician. Not only could she set up the department, she might even head it up for a while.

Udo and I exchanged glances and nodded.

"We'll add a second floor. Then we will not only have a workshop, we can start a proper eye clinic as well!"

I don't know who actually voiced that idea. It might have been Udo, or Michael, or me – or all three of us simultaneously. What I *do* know is at that precise moment, at 10 o'clock in the morning, the Diospi Suyana eye clinic was born.

5

A Great Celebration
with a Side of Stress

Those attending morning devotions that day stared at the veiled shape at the front of the chapel, wondering what might be hidden under the yellow sheet. After the sermon, I invited Udo and Barbara Klemenz to join me at the front. I pulled the sheet away to reveal a bronze plaque.

I read the engraved text aloud: "For civil engineer Udo Klemenz and his wife Barbara, in recognition of their historic contribution in making the dream of Diospi Suyana come true. This couple has dedicated more than three years of their lives to the construction of the Diospi Suyana hospital and dental clinic. We give thanks to God for their excellent service on behalf of the Quechua people."

I looked over at Udo and his wife, pleased to see how moved they were. On 14 April 2010, they would be returning to Germany. Sadly, they would miss the inauguration of the dental and eye clinics, as their flight had been booked months in advance.

Five years previously, this couple had prayed in their kitchen, asking God for a special purpose. Their mission was now complete. Although the formal celebration of the product of their efforts would not take place until June, we honoured them this day as faithful servants of Christ.

There were only eight weeks left until the inauguration, and we continued onwards in relative peace and quiet. To be honest, this is a rare experience at Diospi Suyana. When it does happen, I often wonder if it is merely the calm before another storm!

Amid the cacophony and dust produced by the mad progress of the painters, electricians, and glaziers, the Mörls set up the optical workshop on the first floor of the new building. An enthusiastic optician from Blaufelden, Reinhard Müller, donated the necessary instruments. Despite all the forward momentum, we were still behind schedule.

The staff looked forward to Saturday 26 June with much excitement and anticipation. On the Thursday of that week, a massive articulated lorry strained its way up to the hospital entrance with container number 27. Dr Dankfried Geister, his wife Dorothea, and dentist Erin Connally immediately set to unwrapping the contents of the various pallets. They discovered a quarter of a million dollars' worth of critical supplies, primarily for the dental clinic. Christmas had come early, but just in time.

Not three hours later, Ms Ayla Bloomberg arrived from New York. She would be representing the Henry Schein company at the upcoming festivities. Ms Bloomberg also planned to shoot a short promotional film for her company while in Curahuasi.

A team led by Udo Klemenz got to work hanging the vertical blinds. Yes, you read that correctly – he came back! Udo found himself "homesick" and could not bear to stay in Solms any longer. He made an impulsive decision to return to Peru, and now would be able to share the grand celebration with his Diospi Suyana family in person.

Michael Mörl and another team installed taps donated by the Mexican company Helvex in the dental clinic toilets. Ortrun Heinz directed the kitchen and cleaning crews. These spirited ladies had been preparing for the big event for quite a while and radiated both peace and purpose as they scrubbed and scoured.

Then it was Friday. Katrin Kägler and Ulrike Beck transformed the drab concrete of the amphitheatre into a truly festive setting, using balloons in Peru's national colours. Meanwhile, construction workers cleaned the steps and seats to rid the stadium of black widow spiders. We certainly did not want this momentous occasion to be overshadowed by painful, poisonous bites.

In the morning, a TV crew from Peru's Channel 4 arrived and immediately began to film. The two reporters seemed quite resilient, having just endured the flight from Lima to Cusco and a three-hour car ride up through the mountains. Similarly impressive, the nine musicians of the band Arpay emerged casually from their bus after the nineteen-hour drive from Lima, a journey of more 600 miles.

At 11 a.m. Olaf Böttger, Chairman of Diospi Suyana, Germany, arrived in a taxi shared with Jörg Vogel, a Bolivian entrepreneur from Sirona, and Jürgen Eiskolb, an honorary member of Diospi Suyana.

Graphic designer Manolo Chavez from Cusco had promised to hang signs in the dental clinic the previous Monday. Monday turned into Friday, and Friday turned into midnight. Manolo was never short of excuses, and this time was no exception. I felt my blood pressure spike just looking at him.

As I was writing my news update for the Diospi Suyana website at 11 p.m. that evening, numerous individuals continued to toil in preparation for the celebration that would take place in only a few more hours. The second Diospi Suyana project would be officially opened! With generous donations from sixteen different companies, a luxurious clinic offering high-quality eye and dental care to the poor had been created.

Saturday arrived. In the morning, gynaecologist Dr Jens Hassfeld drove our car to welcome Peruvian First Lady Pilar Nores de García at the airport. A police escort and bodyguards were already waiting in the Arrivals hall. When she appeared, there was momentary confusion, which led to a lapse in protocol. Instead of getting into the special vehicle provided by the police, the First Lady ended up in our car! Dr Hassfeld had the privilege and challenge of chauffeuring the president's wife round the twisting bends of mountain roads. With sweating palms, the gynaecologist gripped the steering wheel and attempted to find clever topics of conversation with which to entertain Pilar Nores for three hours.

Whether it was Dr Hassfeld's driving or the rough terrain, Pilar Nores was as white as a sheet by the time the green Hyundai turned into the back car park of the hospital.

We escorted the president's wife to a small apartment so she could rest for a few hours. This conveniently provided an opportunity for us to investigate the disturbing news we were receiving from the amphitheatre – it was completely empty! Rumours were beginning to circulate as to why. Would we be able to host the celebration with no guests?

Udo Klemenz and I drove into town, hoping to encounter long lines of Curahuasinos marching towards the hospital. The streets of Curahuasi were busy as usual, but no one seemed to be heading in our direction. Back in August 2007, there had

43

been thousands of people at the hospital by lunchtime, ahead of the inauguration. What on earth was going on?

Troubled, we drove back to my house and began to pray. "Oh, God, so many of our staff have put so much effort into making this celebration special. Now it seems there is no one to share our joy. Please help us!"

Pilar Nores emerged at the doorway. It was time for lunch. A delicious fare of soup, roast chicken, and German crumble cake was served in the hospital dining room. Every ten minutes I asked how many visitors were in the amphitheatre.

"About a hundred. No more than that."

My confusion and unease escalated into panic.

We needed to buy some time, so we provided our distinguished guests with a tour of the hospital and dental clinic. Jörg Vogel and Ayla Bloomberg shared the details of their considerable corporate donations with the president's wife.

By about 2 p.m. we reached the amphitheatre with our guests. A great weight lifted and I breathed a deep sigh of relief as I noted approximately 2,500 people in the audience, creating a colourful and very welcome scene. The crowd was ready for the festivities to begin – and so were we. As the cameras from five different TV stations began to roll, local children marched in and a police band played the national anthems of Peru and Germany, as well as the town of Curahuasi's own song.

Then it was time for me to step forward and address the audience. I really dislike formal speeches, unless, of course, they are about what is truly important in life. I gave a brief description of Diospi Suyana, then jumped into what I really wanted to share.

"Diospi Suyana is not a self-sustaining hospital. It is a work of faith, built and run through trust in God. The Holy

Scriptures have told us for thousands of years that we live in the shadow of the Almighty. It is only through God's providence that the Diospi Suyana hospital and dental clinic have been made possible!"

I don't know if you have ever experienced the inauguration of a public building. Usually the speeches are all about the purpose of the building, the hard work of those who did the planning and construction, with perhaps a nod towards external support. God is never mentioned. But things are different here at Diospi Suyana, and God is everything.

"Faith is of no interest to the public, unless, of course, faith is lived out in such a selfless and genuine way that others benefit," I continued. "Serving God and your neighbour costs, and the price can be quite dear. Our most valuable assets here at the hospital are our volunteers, many of whom serve for years, ministering to those forgotten or despised, and showing the truth that God's love changes lives."

I paused and gazed into the crowd before me. Out there were indigenous people and Mestizos from the mountains. They knew all about the hardships of life, the daily struggle for food, clothing, and work. Sickness and death were not theoretical possibilities but harsh and present realities. This is why I had to share the hope that had brought my wife and me to Curahuasi years before.

"For years I wondered if God even existed." I spoke slowly and clearly so the meaning would not be lost. "I wanted to know if there was anything beyond this life, any hope; if the eternal life through Christ I had heard about was actually real. My mother had passed away four months prior. My cousin had passed away three weeks prior, and my uncle two weeks prior. The question 'Does God exist?' became the most

45

important one in my life. Over the years, I have learned that we cannot *prove* the existence of God, but we can certainly experience Him."

I don't know how long my words were remembered by those who heard them that day. But I am sure the folk dance performed by members of the Diospi Suyana staff was not soon forgotten! In the mountains of Peru, a dance performance is a key component of any celebration. Twenty Quechuas, adorned in brightly coloured dress, bounded and whirled in circular formation to the strains of ancient Inca music. Three of our missionaries joined in. One would have had to be blind to miss that Stefan Höfer, Alexandra Kopp, and Marit Weilbach were gringos, despite their elaborate costumes. Nevertheless, the audience rewarded their performance with thunderous applause.

In keeping with a dental theme, several children played the roles of the evil tooth trolls Karius and Baktus, enthusiastically hacking large holes with pickaxes into the huge model teeth centre stage. A giant toothbrush, two metres in length, put an end to the dental destruction, as a visit to the new Diospi Suyana dental clinic was recommended for any audience member suffering from holes in their teeth.

The sun was nearly setting as Pilar Nores de García reached for the scissors to cut the red ribbon in front of thousands of onlookers, with many more viewing later on national TV. To enable everyone to experience this historic event, we symbolically substituted a small model of the dental clinic on a small table near the platform. Our children, Natalie and Dominik, had made it for me as a present the previous Christmas. Now the papier mâché construction became the centre of attention. Pilar Nores stepped forward and cut the ribbon surrounding the model dental clinic, amid flashing cameras and exuberant cheers. The dental clinic that had taken two years to build was now open for treatment.

Not four days later, the celebrations long over, we found ourselves planning yet another phase of Diospi Suyana. In a small office at the hospital, my wife and I sat with Michael Mörl and an Australian named Lyndal Maxwell. We listened closely as a man wearing a T-shirt sporting the logo "Dieter's Sports Group" in large letters explained his brother-in-law's architectural design for the construction of a Children's House to accommodate the Diospi Suyana Kids' Clubs.

In April 2010, we had been able to acquire a 700 m^2 (7500 sq ft) plot of land in the middle of Curahuasi for a reasonable price, and we now intended to build a three-storey house there. On the ground floor, there would be three large rooms, a kitchen, and some toilets – an ideal location for the Kids' Clubs. Four small apartments on the first floor and two larger ones on the second floor would provide much-needed accommodation for missionary families.

The man from "Dieter's Sports Group" was so enthusiastic about the plans, you might have thought he was building the house himself. In my report for the website I didn't want to give away his identity. But I had to admit, from behind he bore a striking resemblance to a certain Udo Klemenz....

GOD HAS SEEN US

6

The Building Comes to Life

Dr Erin Connally, from the US state of Washington, and her team of assistants began treating their first patients in the dental clinic in July 2010. But she was not to operate on her own for long. Soon she was joined by both Peruvian and short-term missionary dentists. Tibor Minge, from Oranienburg, Germany, assumed responsibility for setting up and running the dental lab for a year. Tibor is a man with extraordinary drive and energy. While others retreated to their homes at 5 p.m., worn out after a full day's work, Tibor stayed to teach karate and self-defence to local children. It was such a joy to watch them fly through the air as they practised the different skills Tibor was teaching them.

The five donated dental chairs could adequately accommodate the needs of at least three dentists, but I knew it would be a challenge to grow our dental team. In the West, dentists are extremely well paid. The security and comfort of a substantial income often makes it difficult for anyone to consider volunteering as a missionary.

For hundreds of years, the number of doctors and dentists serving worldwide in the mission field at any given point in time has been approximately a thousand. This is barely a drop in the ocean, considering the vast need. In German-speaking countries alone there are half a million doctors and dentists. In English-speaking countries there are significantly more than

GOD HAS SEEN US

2 million. But who is willing to leave the perks and prestige behind in order to serve sacrificially at a mission hospital? That takes a special soul with very personal motivation.

Dr Marlen Luckow is one such soul. On 27 March 2012 I sat opposite this Swiss national in a café at the Freiburg train station. The pretty dentist from Basel shared her story with me, taking me back in time to 2002.

Marlen Luckow is just eighteen years old. She has been feeling unwell for weeks. A visit to the doctor and a series of tests reveal the devastating reason behind her ill health: Marlen has Hodgkin's lymphoma. Stage 4.

Is this it? she wonders. *Is my life already over?*

Refusing to accept what appears to be inevitable, Marlen decides instead to fight, finding strength in her faith. Multiple rounds of chemotherapy leave her too weak to stand, requiring friends to carry her up the stairs to her house. For six gruelling months, she is ripped from the life she has known, with no idea whether or not she will ultimately survive.

But she did.

"Dr Luckow, am I right in supposing that volunteering at our clinic is perhaps your way of saying thank you to God?"

"Yes," she nods. "You could say that."

With the dental clinic now up and running at capacity, we turned our attention to the staffing needs of the eye clinic. We were joined by Dr Ursula Buck from Augsburg. She had heard the name Diospi Suyana several times over the years but had never been inspired to dig deeper. She felt the concept was idealistic. How could the hospital sustain such high-quality care to the poor on a long-term basis? Dr Buck herself had previously served as a missionary in Africa. She was no stranger to the hardship, obsolete or absent equipment, and crippling lack of financial resources common in medical centres in developing countries.

Dr Buck would never have dreamed of purchasing my book about Diospi Suyana. If she had happened to receive it as a gift, I have no doubt it would have collected dust on a shelf somewhere. Diospi Suyana was simply not her thing.

One day in August 2010, her friend Renate Reibold visited Dr Buck at her apartment in Augsburg.

"Ursula," she exclaimed, "I've just read the most amazing book – you've *got* to read it!"

Dr Buck's gaze fell on the title: *I Have Seen God: Diospi Suyana – the Hospital of Hope*. She frowned, uninterested.

"You know what? I'll just leave the book here with you!" Renate offered. "When you come to visit me in October, you can return it to me then."

Dr Buck sighed. There was always some external pressure to cope with, pushing in one direction or another. She would need to at least skim through the book so as not to disappoint her friend, who would no doubt want to discuss it during their next visit.

One evening, Dr Buck finally relented and began to read. She could not put the book down, fascinated by the Diospi Suyana story. The subsequent chapter of her life could be titled "What Happens When You Try to Be Polite", as Dr Buck has headed up our eye clinic since 2012!

Her very first operation was on a Quechua man who had been gored in the eye by an angry bull. With the aid of a new surgical microscope by Haag-Streit, Dr Buck was able to save the man's sight. An impressive debut indeed!

In the first eight years of operation, more than 50,000 patients were treated in our dental and eye clinics. With very few exceptions, the equipment utilized in both clinics is brand new, state of the art, and generously donated by large companies. Its value exceeds $600,000. Every time I walk into the clinic, I am overwhelmed by gratitude.

I think our patients feel the same way.

7

We Become Peruvians

A functioning mission hospital can quickly become an object of great envy. Diospi Suyana is well equipped, clean, efficient, and locally in high demand. It would only be logical for the government to step in and secure such a valuable resource, deporting the foreign missionaries. Such a nightmare has played out repeatedly in other countries, where what has been established in the name and love of Christ at great personal sacrifice is destroyed with a single government directive. We were concerned that it could happen to Diospi Suyana too. What could we do to decrease this unthinkable risk?

I began to consider that my wife and I should apply to become Peruvian citizens. If we did so, there would then be no possibility of being deported. My position as the chairman of Diospi Suyana – Peru would then make the hospital a Peruvian corporation, but one with Peruvian leadership.

In early 2009 I made initial enquiries at the Immigration Department in Lima. The government worker assisting me, Gladys Barboza, demanded bluntly, "How much money do you earn here in Peru?"

"My wife and I receive financial gifts from a number of supporters in Germany," I responded delicately.

"That won't work. You have to earn a salary in this country or you will never be able to obtain citizenship."

Pressing for a more reasonable response and solution, we soon found ourselves in the midst of a circular argument. I told her about Diospi Suyana. I pulled press reports from my bag and shared an abbreviated presentation of our work on my laptop.

"Incredible!" exclaimed Ms Barboza, clearly moved. She added, "In this case, you should be awarded honorary citizenship for outstanding services to our nation."

I nodded gratefully. "How does that work?"

Ms Barboza promised her assistance in getting this accomplished. Had I known then how ridiculously long and difficult the process was going to be, I probably would have given up right there.

Ms Barboza arranged an initial appointment for me with the head of Immigration. I attempted to impress upon him the impact of our work, sharing a few photos on my laptop. Ms Barboza became my cheerleader, emphatically stating, "The Johns deserve honorary citizenship for this!"

The Head of Immigration voiced no objections and forwarded my application to the Ministry of the Interior. I understand that all things take time, particularly in government, but after weeks of no response, I was becoming discouraged.

Ms Barboza came to the rescue once again and arranged an audience for me with Dr Suzy Villegas at the Ministry of the Interior. Dr Villegas was a high-ranking civil servant with significant influence regarding citizenship applications. She requested that I share the Diospi Suyana story with her in detail. Ms Barboza attended as well.

When I had finished, Ms Barboza entreated, "Dr Villegas, after what you have just seen, surely the Johns deserve honorary citizenship?"

Dr Villegas nodded. "Absolutely. I will personally present this request to the Minister of the Interior himself."

And so began the long and winding road through many departments of the Ministry. Whenever I thought our file must surely have been lost, it would suddenly reappear. One day, the Minister signed the necessary document. I learned later that he had consulted with a lawyer, Elena Juscamaita, who advised him to sign, after careful investigation of relevant legislation.

My file was then sent to the Council of Ministers, where it ultimately landed on the desk of President Alan García. President García had already made our acquaintance when we were invited to his palace on 26 April 2008. And his wife, Pilar Nores de García, was of course a prominent supporter of Diospi Suyana. He did not hesitate, and happily graced the document with his signature, then sent it on to Congress.

This is where everything stopped cold. Nothing happened, nothing moved, and nobody did anything about it.

In my need, I turned to Robert Hernán Seminario, personal legal counsel to the president himself. He was more than willing to help. A few phone calls resulted in an audience with the head of Congress, Dr Alva Castro.

Dr Castro received us on 20 April 2010. He sat at his desk in an elegant office, allowing me to set up my laptop on a table, next to his files.

Only fifteen minutes into my presentation, Dr Castro became a believer in our work.

"We should have voted on your case long ago. Tomorrow you will have an opportunity to present your petition on the Congressional Floor."

There is a saying in Peru: "Everybody can move quickly when it is too late." Fortunately, it wasn't too late, but things definitely started to move.

Indeed, the very next day I found myself before twenty leading statesmen. I was allocated little time, yet I managed to click through a hundred photos in a flash presentation, emphasizing throughout that God was the true architect behind Diospi Suyana, not us.

The following afternoon I was on my way back to Curahuasi. The sun cast a deep red glow across the landscape as it began to set.

My mobile rang. It was a member of Dr Alva Castro's staff.

"Dr John, can you get to a TV? Your honorary citizenship was just presented to Congress and they will be voting in a few minutes!"

The vote was unanimous across party lines. The Congress of the Republic of Peru officially decreed that my wife and I would be awarded honorary citizenship for outstanding service to the people of Peru. We were told that such a declaration is only made, on average, once every five years.

I find this story remarkable. We only asked for citizenship, like any other immigrant. But in the end, the Council of Ministers, Congress, and the president himself came together and we were honoured in a session of Congress, broadcast live in Peru on Channel 7.

Every time my wife and I cross the border of Peru, an icon of the Peruvian flag appears next to our names on the immigration official's monitor. We cannot be deported. We are as free as the Peruvian national anthem declares.

But what of our German citizenship? We retain that as well, thanks to special approval from the Foreign Office in Berlin.

The John family has five members. My wife and I are now official citizens of Peru. Natalie was born in South Africa, and is eligible for South African citizenship, should she so choose. Florian was born in Ecuador and would have no difficulty obtaining an Ecuadorian passport from Quito. Only our son Dominik is a true-blue, genuine German. And of that he can be proud.

8

The Most Famous
Lift in the World

It has become almost a daily occurrence. Guests arrive unannounced at the entrance of the hospital, hoping to come inside. The old Inca capital of Cuzco is only two and a half hours away from Curahuasi, so it makes perfect sense for tourists to visit not only Machu Picchu but Diospi Suyana as well. Visitors might arrive alone by dusty taxi or in groups by coach. Occasionally, we get advance notice, but not often. Regardless of their home language, our guests from all over the world are able to communicate their request: to look around the Diospi Suyana hospital.

Whenever possible during the working week, we personally walk the interested tourists through the various hospital departments. This visual first impression stays with them long after their departure, and often grows into the desire to financially support the hospital or share the story of Diospi Suyana in their home towns. As the Bible says, when God's word goes out, it never, ever returns empty.

On 15 July 2010, the Schreier family arrived on our doorstep. They impatiently shoved open the car doors to stretch their tired and aching legs. But this group had more on their minds than a three-hour tour. Wolf-Dietrich Schreier, his wife Kerstin, son Hans, and friend Karin would be sacrificially spending three weeks of their annual leave on a special mission. They firmly intended to continue one of the most thrilling chapters in Diospi Suyana history – one that had begun eighteen months earlier in the Ore Mountains of Germany.

I can still remember our Starbucks stop at Lima airport. Tina and I were just about to board the plane home to Germany with our children. The flight would take twelve hours, and there would be no time for jetlag; we would be celebrating Christmas with our parents the very next day. I cradled my frappuccino in my right hand, as my left was still sore from a car accident the week before. We planned to "recover" as a family somewhere in the Ore Mountains.

We hadn't yet booked any accommodation, so I took advantage of our coffee break to set up my laptop rather awkwardly on the table. Tina began to type in the search engine: "winter break", "holiday apartments". Almost instantly, the screen was filled with photos of snow-covered dwellings and promises of a refreshing holiday.

As usual, everything was a bit last minute with the Johns. We still had to get through passport control and security.

"Ooh, that one looks really nice," my wife noted, pointing to a small, gingerbread-like house. I leaned over to see the details. It was located in the small town of Eibenstock, which meant nothing to us at the time. But it was affordable and available, so there we were: our holiday in the mountains of Saxony all sorted.

"Now we have to run for it!" I yelled to the children as we grabbed our bags and dashed to the departure gate.

We were not to regret our stay in Eibenstock. We felt a sense of peace and satisfaction as we approached the enchanting two-storey house with its snowy garden. Our last-minute booking of Gabelsbergstraße 9 turned out to be a winner. We picked up the keys from the landlady next door and made ourselves at home.

The next morning, I paid the landlady another visit – this time with an awkward request. I took a deep breath.

"Frau Schreier," I began tentatively, "I have to update my website every day. Would it be possible to use your internet connection while we are here?"

Frau Schreier was aware that my wife and I were missionary doctors in Peru, and no doubt guessed that we were not her average tenants.

"No problem at all," she replied graciously. "What kind of website is it?"

Since I had my laptop with me, there was no reason not to share our story then and there. Forty-five minutes later, I had once again presented the miracle of Diospi Suyana. As always, my enthusiasm grew as I worked my way through the slides, and this time it was clearly contagious. Frau Schreier and her son Hans had never heard of Diospi Suyana before, but were captivated by the incredible tale of providence and "coincidence".

Even the best of holidays must come to an end. My wife and I returned to the Schreier residence to settle the balance of our required payment. We owed about €800, to be paid in cash.

As we offered the money, Herr and Frau Schreier declined in unison. "We don't want your money. Please accept your holiday here as a gift from us. We would be delighted if you could join us for dinner this evening before you go."

Tina and I have perfected the "poker face" in response to a fair number of surprises in our lives, but we were completely caught off guard by the Schreiers' extraordinary generosity.

Of course we would accept their kind invitation. It was not only the children who enjoyed the delicious spaghetti. As we relaxed in the cosy living room for some after-dinner conversation, we quickly progressed into animated discourse.

Herr Schreier was just sharing an exciting experience, when he mentioned in passing that he used to work for a lift company. The word "lift" hit me like lightning.

"A lift!" I exclaimed. "That is just what we need at our hospital." My thoughts quickly turned to the empty shaft that we would love to fill with a working lift, if only a benefactor could be found.

As we were headed back to Wiesbaden the next morning, the lift idea became a priority for the Schreier family. Our holiday landlords were determined to find a way, through their contacts in the business, to acquire a lift for the Diospi Suyana hospital.

Lo and behold, from February 2009 a stream of emails and phone calls flowed between Curahuasi and Eibenstock. I learned that a lift has multiple components. There is obviously the cabin, where passengers stand. You also need doors, a strong motor, tracks, counterweights, and a reliable electrical system of considerable power. Steel cables and emergency fittings complete the list of required equipment.

Not much movement occurred until 13 July, when I received a very promising message from Herr Schreier: "Dr John, it has been a while and we hope that you and your family are doing well. I wanted to make sure you knew that there will be a lift trade expo in Augsburg this October. You would be able to meet representatives from all of the lift companies in the world, including the ones I have recommended to you. If you can get here, this could be an invaluable opportunity, and would save you lots of time and money in the long run. I would be more than happy to go with you!"

He was on! I would fly from Peru for a possibility such as this without hesitation. After all, it was for the good of our hospital. For Wolf-Dietrich Schreier to drive from Saxony to Augsburg was no small feat, and I was once again humbled by the generosity of this man. What did he have to do with Diospi Suyana? Nothing really. Five strangers, making up my family, booked a holiday at his guest house, invaded his office every day, and left him nothing but dirty spaghetti plates.

If you are thinking that all of this came from the Schreiers' sense of Christian duty or conviction, you could not be more wrong. Wolf-Dietrich and Kerstin grew up under an atheist regime in East Germany. When the Berlin Wall finally came down, they began to explore spirituality, finding comfort in the New Age movement, the beliefs of which are distinctly different from the teachings of Christ.

It was 15 October 2009, and my birthday. A cold front was advancing through southern Bavaria, snowflakes swirling far too early through the frosty air. Although we had no connection to any of the lift-manufacturing companies, somehow we were granted access to the massive exhibition hall. Wolf-Dietrich knew precisely what we needed: nine components for a lift that would carry a bed. My mission was to "sell" the vision of Diospi Suyana to the various vendors, in the hope that they might respond with a crucial donation.

Armed with flyers and brochures, we picked our way through the teeming crowds. Wolf-Dietrich steered me straight towards the companies that could supply what we needed for our lift. The total cost of what we required

61

GOD HAS SEEN US

approached $50,000. Our plan to solicit donations to this sum was bold, and highly unlikely to meet with success. Reason enough for me to send up some silent prayers as we made our rounds!

The most expensive part of a lift is the motor, which can cost up to $10,000, depending on the size. In search of a motor, we found ourselves at the Ziehl-Abegg stand, a brand name that represents top quality. We spoke briefly with the staff manning the display, but since their boss was not present, we arranged a meeting with him for 2 p.m. We left behind some of our literature in case there might be an opportunity for him to peruse it prior to speaking with us in person.

When we returned that afternoon, company representatives were expecting us. They asked us to wait briefly until Herr Arnold, an authorized executive of the Künzelsau-based firm, could speak with us directly.

As he turned his attention to us, Herr Arnold appeared friendly enough, but also extremely busy and not particularly patient with idle chatter. He greeted us, then immediately jumped to the subject of our request.

"When my staff told me earlier that I needed to speak with some people from Peru who wanted me to give them a motor for free, I thought they had lost their minds. I mean, really! We are a business and we have better things to do than simply give away our products to anyone who asks."

Herr Arnold paused and seemed to consider his next words very carefully. I got the feeling I was going to hear something completely unexpected.

"I opened your brochure," Herr Arnold continued, "and saw the very same hospital my brother-in-law visited in Peru last year. He showed us photos of it in our living room. He was so enthusiastic – I just knew immediately we had to do something to help."

And that was that. I laughed out loud. Another crazy story. Herr Arnold hadn't really wanted to help us, but there was this strange "coincidence" involving his brother-in-law, and suddenly his position was reversed. These acts of providence are impossible for those without faith to understand. CEOs and journalists scratch their heads, perplexed. Since they do not believe in the power of prayer, they have no explanation when miracles occur at Diospi Suyana.

What a birthday! Wolf-Dietrich and I were feeling more optimistic by the hour. There might have been an icy wind blustering outside, but our hearts glowed warm with hope inside.

In time, it was done. Our mission had been fully accomplished. A Hungarian company, Merico, had pledged to provide all the plans and equipment needed for the lift shaft. Omeras GmbH of Lautern, offered to construct the cabin free of charge. The electrical controls and operating gear would be supplied by Schneider of Hilzingen. Riedl would donate the doors, and Sautter of Stuttgart the counterweights and emergency cabin framework. But it was the motor from Ziehl-Abegg that was the icing on the cake for me.

Towards the end of that evening, I sat opposite Frau Götz, reporter for the *Lift Report* trade journal. She had surely never encountered such a large charitable endowment given so quickly! In March 2010, the journal published three pages in German and two in English, detailing the incredible story of our lift acquisition. In July of the same year, another three-page article appeared in the Argentinian magazine *Revista del*

63

Ascensor. There are thousands of lifts in the world. Nobody thinks much about them as they step in and press the button for their desired floor. But our lift is famous. There is no lift that has received the extensive press coverage that ours has here at Diospi Suyana.

The Schreiers had travelled all the way to Peru for the express purpose of assembling and installing our newly acquired lift. Michael Mörl lent his technical expertise as a qualified mill constructor. As he also hails from Saxony, there were no communication difficulties whatsoever as they laboured together through this monumental task.

The lift can transport twenty-one people, or loads of up to 1.6 tonnes. The gentlemen from our logistics department use it daily as they transport loads of heavy boxes. And when we opened the second floor for patient care in 2016, the lift was a blessing to everyone. Should we ever expand the first floor to increase ward space, we will already have the solution for moving the patients' beds.

9

A Desperate Search

It is impossible to delve into the history of Diospi Suyana without coming across the name Michael Mörl. That said, Michael has never been one to push himself into the spotlight. He is a rather quiet man, unremarkably dressed. To say that he exudes a "magnetic personality" would be a bit of an overstatement, but he is certainly one of a kind.

Michael hails from Gaußig, near Bautzen, in Saxony. Prior to joining the Diospi Suyana team, he was employed as a nurse at the Cardiac Centre in Dresden. He and his wife Elisabeth were busy raising five children in a charming country cottage.

He spent three and a half years at Diospi Suyana. He spent as much time in intensive care and the operating theatre as he did in the workshops. He was quite literally all over the place, sometimes making it a challenge to find him. But he was always working, often seventy or eighty hours each week. Nobody asked him to do this; he just followed his heart and his principles. If ever he saw something that needed doing, he took care of it.

Michael grew up in former East Germany. His parents were Christians, a rare breed in a self-declared atheistic country. Their faith required bravery and true conviction. When the Mörls applied to work with Diospi Suyana back in 2006, he shared the following story from his childhood – a key experience that cemented his belief in the existence of God.

Michael was eleven years old at the time. One afternoon, he fancied a ride on their horse, Susan. His mother gave her permission and off he went. He knew he would need a riding crop, and seeing his brother's new one hanging on the stable wall, he grabbed it before climbing into the saddle.

That is when the trouble started. Susan was normally quite a calm horse, but not this day. She suddenly broke into a full gallop, crashing across a paddock and through a fence on the other side. Michael panicked and threw himself off the horse, miraculously without injury. He managed to catch up with Susan but could not bring himself to mount again, given her recent behaviour. He walked her all the way back home, leading her by the bridle, the crop carefully secured under the saddle.

Michael took a shortcut, leading the horse through a cornfield. Several threshers clattered up and down the large field, reaping the harvest of corn.

At long last, Michael arrived home. He went to hang the riding crop back up on the wall, but it was gone.

"Mama," Michael called sheepishly, "I can't find the riding crop."

"Michael, you get back out there right now!" his mother scolded. "That riding crop belongs to your brother and cost a lot of money. You had better find it."

The boy grabbed his bicycle and set out again. He rode up and down shaded paths, sweeping his gaze continually from side to side, hoping to see the crop. But to no avail. He had a sinking feeling that the crop was somewhere in the middle of that cornfield with the threshers. He had no idea what to do. He did know he would never be able to find it in that huge field. But he couldn't go home empty-handed. What could he do? Maybe God could help him.

Michael took his hands off the handlebars and folded them in prayer. He closed his eyes, remembering that his pastor had told him it was better to pray that way so he wouldn't get distracted. Michael took a deep breath.

"Oh, God, I'll never find the riding crop. The field is way too big. I don't know what else to do. Please help me!"

He opened his eyes and prepared to ride on. Then he saw it, in the brush directly in front of him – the riding crop.

Michael has never forgotten that answered prayer. It continues to give him the courage to come to Jesus with a childlike trust, just as the disciples were told to 2,000 years ago.

Three decades have passed since that day, but Michael can still recall exactly how he felt standing on the edge of that field: first afraid, then depressed, then overjoyed. For sure, he had found the expensive riding crop, but more than that, he had found faith in a living God.

I spend about half of every year on the road, sharing the story of Diospi Suyana with clubs, schools, companies, and so on. I meet the most fascinating people who have stories of their own to share with me. All the stories, including this one from Michael Mörl, have one thing in common: they all testify to the reality of our loving Lord and Father.

10

Perfect Timing

Good dental care is expensive. The lack of such care for those without financial means should cause humanity to feel shame. In Europe and the United States, people can generally afford decent dental work. But in developing countries, people either go without or take their chances on a quack who has neither skill nor proper equipment.

Tibor Minge set up the dental lab, leaving nothing undone. He very prudently even thought of outfitting the lab with a CAD CAM machine, which creates perfect ceramic dentures through a computer-assisted procedure. We learned there were only four such machines in all of Peru. Three were located in upscale clinics in Lima. The fourth, to our patients' utter delight, was with us!

Tibor had committed to working with Diospi Suyana for one year. He planned to return to Germany in May 2012. How could we possibly replace him? In addition to having enormous shoes to fill, it is not as though we could order missionaries from a catalogue or entice them with a generous salary and benefits packages. No, we need very special people who hear God's call on their lives and who are prepared to face great challenges.

Being called by God sounds a bit mystical – maybe something experienced by people in another age, or perhaps even a figment of the imagination. It's one thing to accept that God exists. It's quite another to believe that He is actively involved in each of our lives, because, as one particularly sceptical man dismissed the idea, "Then God would really be busy." His personal view was that the concept of "divine intervention" had more to do with wishful thinking than reality.

At this point, I would like to introduce Lisa Isaak. Lisa spent the first six years of her life in Kazakhstan, a country bordered by the Caspian Sea on the west and the Altai Mountains on the east. There was a population of approximately 17 million prior to the collapse of the Soviet Union. After Kazakhstan declared independence in 1990, 2 million people, predominantly Germans and Russians, left the country. Lisa remembers her parents selling their home in exchange for goods, as the emigrants were not allowed to take large sums of money with them.

For Lisa, the next chapter of her life was in Michelstadt, Hesse. After finishing school, she took a job as a sales associate in a meat market. But she wanted to do more. She began a three-year dental technician course and was surprised to discover her own aptitude for creating dentures. She was thrilled to have found her "niche".

Lisa could easily have found work and stayed in Germany, but deep within she felt she belonged elsewhere. As a Christian, she desperately wanted to share her gifts with those who truly needed help and couldn't afford it. A noble calling indeed, but she just couldn't find a suitable job. Because of the horrendous expense involved with making and fitting dentures, it was nearly impossible to find a missionary dental lab that would provide such a service for free.

But Lisa refused to give up. She exhausted every search engine on the internet. Nothing. She asked everyone she knew. Again, nothing. A year and a half passed, and she was no nearer to her goal. She had prayed regularly that God would give her direction, but she still felt quite uncertain of her path.

Some people think praying is just another term for meditation, perhaps having some therapeutic benefit but no real *power*. We vent our frustrations and pain, reflect on our lives, consider important decisions. All probably useful, but does anyone actually *hear*? Sceptics might say that ceilings don't prevent God from hearing – because He is not there anyway. Since Richard Dawkins wrote *The God Delusion*, it has been increasingly accepted that God is simply a fictional character.

Lisa had not read Dawkins' book, but she was very familiar with God's word, in which it says that He not only hears our prayers, He also answers in His way and in His time. So this young lady made a pivotal decision: if she could not find a missionary post in her chosen career field, she would find another career field. She resolved to retrain as a nurse. Lisa was willing to invest another three years of her life solely for the opportunity to volunteer at a mission hospital. I know few others who would make such a sacrifice.

In early 2011, Lisa applied to three German hospitals as a nursing trainee. By Easter, she had been accepted by a hospital in Stuttgart. She had a decision to make. Yet something still did not feel right. Perhaps she was suspicious of her own courage? Lisa has always been very solid and practical, not one to chase after whimsy. She knew what everyone would advise her to do: stay in Germany; earn a respectable salary working as a dental technician in Germany. You don't have to go overseas – just send money.

70

Lisa pondered and prayed, and prayed and pondered. Suddenly, she recalled a moment many months previously. Didn't somebody once tell her something about a mission hospital somewhere in South America? She put Google to work and found herself on the Diospi Suyana website.

The daily update for that particular day, 27 April 2011, read: "Diospi Suyana Dental Clinic Treats Orphans from Urubamba!" As Lisa read on, she could feel her heart beating faster. On the very day she found the website, the dental clinic was at the forefront. The story was accompanied by a picture of our dental clinic, nearly indistinguishable from any modern practice in Europe.

Lisa contacted our German office immediately. She received a friendly, but not particularly helpful, response. She was told about an information meeting for prospective volunteers that would take place on 9 July.

At the beginning of May, Lisa received an employment contract from the hospital in Stuttgart, to be signed and returned within two weeks. The contract lay on Lisa's desk. She had two weeks to make possibly the most important decision of her life. The time flew by.

By 22 May 2011, the two-week response window was closed. That Sunday evening, Lisa knew she could not delay any longer. Waiting until the July info day was simply too long. So with a heavy heart, she flipped through the pages of the contract until she reached the signature page at the back. She sighed deeply as she wrote her name in the space provided. This wasn't what she wanted. It wasn't a dental technician position at a mission hospital. Life sometimes isn't ideal. Life sometimes isn't clear. Nobody escapes the detours, the mistakes, the defeats – not even Lisa. She had been waiting for God's clear direction for more than a year, but it hadn't come.

She put her pen down and glanced at her laptop. A new email had just popped up from somebody named Klaus John. She opened the message and could scarcely believe her eyes. It read: "What is your phone number? I would like to talk to you."

So the next day I had a long conversation with Lisa and invited her to Curahuasi. The signed contract for Stuttgart landed in the bin, and on 1 February 2012 she arrived in Lima. Here at Diospi Suyana, Lisa has been able to follow her calling, and experiences deep satisfaction in doing so. For three years she served the Quechua people and, in that process, God Himself. As Jesus says in Matthew 25:40, "Whatever you did for one of the least of these brothers and sisters of mine, you did for me." (NIV)

What made me email Lisa on that particular day? I have no idea. I didn't know her personally. I must have heard of her enquiry a few days beforehand. Sometimes I am the one who contacts those interested in working with us; sometimes the ladies of the German office reach out. I cannot tell you why on that Sunday I was looking at Lisa's application and subsequently contacted her.

It was quite simply God's perfect timing.

11

At the End of Our Rope

I had never met the woman on the other end of the phone, but what she said made me think.

"Dr John, it is so exciting to hear how Diospi Suyana came to be," she gushed. "But it is even more exciting that it is still in operation."

Her statement was not devoid of logic. "Beginnings" are exciting. Actually creating something on the waves of faith and fellowship does seem to work. People want to be a part of it. Various organizations, private citizens, and whoever else will often pull together to help. Thousands of proverbial hands place one stone on top of another for the satisfaction of seeing it complete. This was certainly the case for Diospi Suyana between 2004 and 2009. There were tears of joy all over the world when the mission hospital was formally opened. What had been said to be impossible had become a reality. Even people without a Christian faith shared our deep sense of gratitude.

"Sustaining", however, is quite another matter. It is the long haul, with no end in sight, the attention and novelty having faded away, perhaps having even been replaced by the next new idea. Sustaining Diospi Suyana is not an easy task. Our poverty-stricken patients pay only about 30 per cent of the actual expenses. The rest is covered by donations and supporters of the missionaries whose salaries we do not pay.

Many may ask how long we can continue in this manner. It currently costs approximately $130,000 per month to operate the components of Diospi Suyana. We do not solicit financial donations through our newsletter or during my presentations. We believe God will move in people's hearts, showing them to what extent, if any, they should become involved. Not exactly a conventional approach to fundraising!

As Diospi Suyana grew from dream into reality, we received donations of high-quality equipment. But nothing lasts forever, and even the most sophisticated devices would need to be replaced one day. I was dreading that day.

In the spring of 2007, Siemens donated a CT scanner under the most remarkable of circumstances. We had heard that this was the first donation of its type to be given by Siemens to South America. When the head of Siemens – Peru, Stefano Garvin, was asked about it during a televised interview during the Diospi Suyana inauguration, he smiled into the camera and declared, "I really love the fact that we are providing the most advanced technology for the poorest people."

While that statement was a hit with the media, it was not entirely true. They had given us an older model, no longer in production. It was not new, but refurbished by the company. Nevertheless, it was of great value to our mission and used by more than 3,000 patients.

In the first week of June 2013, the CT scanner went "on strike". It simply stopped working. Christian Oswald from IT and Markus Rolli, our medical technician, did their best to figure out what had gone wrong. The Siemens technicians arrived. The telephone line to Siemens in Germany was practically on fire. Nothing helped. Our CT remained inoperable. The fault was somewhere in the hardware or software – the technicians were able to narrow it down at least *that* far. But at the end of the day, no spare parts or software programs remained available for obsolete machines. While we are always grateful for donations, this is one of the reasons I advocate for only new equipment to be given to our mission hospital.

A Dr Stephan Feldhaus had been the one to convince Professor Reinhard, the head of Siemens Healthcare, of the benefits of donating a CT scanner. Six years later, I re-established communication with Dr Feldhaus, who by then was one of the directors of the Roche Healthcare company in Switzerland. I met with Dr Feldhaus, his wife, and his son Lukas for lunch and shared the latest photos of Diospi Suyana as we chatted.

"That is fantastic!" declared Dr Feldhaus. "We do have a question to ask you, related to our family."

I had a sense of what was coming – why else would seventeen-year-old Lukas be sitting at the table with us?

"Could our son please volunteer for a year at the hospital?"

They were most pleased with my response.

Lukas Feldhaus was part of the Diospi Suyana team from 2012 to 2013. He carried out assigned duties in administration competently, and helped out with the Kids' Clubs, where his skill in impersonation kept the children roaring with laughter. Even adults guffawed in response to one particular portrayal of an angel. We all had a lot of fun with this intelligent lad from Basle. He was a bright kid, and he was aware of our difficulties with the CT scanner.

"Klaus, just call my dad!" he advised me one morning. "Maybe he can help with the CT – he does know lots of people!"

I looked at Lukas. I knew he was right. "Yes, I will," I responded eagerly. "Give me your parents' phone number."

Stephan Feldhaus went to great lengths to help us out. He made several calls to Professor Requardt, the new head of Siemens Healthcare. Dr Feldhaus also tried to win over Michael Sigmund, who had replaced him as head of communications. Dr Feldhaus knew the needs of Diospi Suyana perhaps better than anyone at that point, both through his son and through his own personal visit to the hospital. His knowledge inspired persistence. After many long and frequent phone calls to Professor Requardt, the professor agreed to donate a brand new, state-of-the-art CT scanner.

I was overjoyed and could scarcely contain my excitement as I prepared a breaking-news article for the website: "Siemens Donates Replacement CT Machine to Hospital!" Six years previously, I had posted the news of the original donation.

But a gift isn't yours until it is actually received. Even the most generous of gifts or the most noble of promises can get stuck along the way. Sometimes an offer is simply forgotten. Or a more senior executive reverses a decision made by an underling. Or the cargo ship disappears forever in the Bermuda Triangle while en route to South America. But those are rare occurrences. A much more common complication is that the Customs Office in Lima decides to confiscate the donation for no comprehensible reason.

In the case of the anticipated scanner, no difficulties were reported – we just failed to receive it within the expected timeframe. A conversation between Dr Feldhaus and Professor Requardt later clarified the reason for this. Professor Requardt and Mr Sigmund had checked out the Diospi Suyana website. They saw that we were a work of faith, fully reliant on God. They were atheists. So they decided not to support the hospital after all.

Despite the fact that Diospi Suyana had been lauded in the press worldwide, and the president himself had invited us to the palace, the realization that we were professing Christians caused great suspicion. Despite the fact that thousands of poor people desperate for help would now not receive it, an ideological difference moved Professor Requardt to withdraw his original offer.

What is a promise worth if you don't believe there is a higher authority to hold you accountable? Richard Dawkins, prominent modern atheist, asserts in his book *Out of Eden*:

> *In a universe of electrons and selfish genes, blind physical forces and genetic replication, some people are going to get hurt, other people are going to get lucky, and you won't find any rhyme or reason in it, nor any justice. The universe that we observe has precisely the properties we should expect if there is, at bottom, no design, no purpose, no evil, no good, nothing but pitiless indifference. DNA neither cares nor knows. DNA just is. And we dance to its music.*

As a Christian, I would agree that this is true – in the absence of a living, loving God. Without God, there is indeed no justice, no good or evil, and in the end there is simply cruel indifference. Sounds like hell to me....

The dream of a replacement CT scanner from Siemens dissolved as quickly as a mirage in the desert. Christian Oswald resumed his attempts to revive our existing CT; it was a problem that appeared completely unsolvable. He became a poster child for perpetual frustration, digging endlessly through circuit diagrams and software programs with zero success.

But then, on 21 October, he miraculously got the CT working again. And just as a VIP was touring our hospital too! Professor Ludwig Georg Braun, honorary president of the German Chamber of Commerce and Industry, was able to witness the scanner in action. It was almost too good to be true.

For such dedication and perseverance, there was no doubt that Christian deserved the Diospi Suyana gold Medal of Honour. I planned to present this award to him – on a red ribbon – immediately following morning devotions on 4 November.

At 8:30 that Monday morning, with the ceremony to begin in just a few minutes, Christian was nowhere to be found. Nobody had seen him in the auditorium and he was not upstairs on the balcony. I looked hurriedly through the corridors and found him in the hospital server room, frantically working to restore our computer system, which had gone down just minutes before.

With a great deal of persuasion, I managed to extricate Christian from the world of cables, currents, and hard drives long enough for him to receive his well-earned award, the Diospi Suyana 2013 Medal of Honour. He stood there shyly for all of about three minutes before scurrying back to the server room, his medal bouncing off his chest, to complete the necessary repairs. I suspected he was already a contender for the 2014 Medal of Honour with such effort!

We were fully aware that we were only buying time. We urgently needed a new CT scanner, because sooner or later ours would irreparably break down. I met with a representative of Siemens in Germany, hoping to perhaps negotiate a deal with a junior manager. A used version of the CT scanner we had been offered would cost €200,000 – a huge amount of money for a mission hospital dependent on donations for day-to-day functioning. It would be a real challenge to come up with that kind of money. But the solution to our need was already on its way.

In Germany, there is an organization called ProChrist, which regularly hosts outreach events to those who do not know Jesus. In addition to sharing the gospel, another significant benefit is that Christians of all denominations come together to make these events happen.

Such an event was planned for the first week of March 2013, to take place at the Porsche Arena in Stuttgart. Some 800 Catholic and Protestant churches would be participating, either in person or via satellite, creating a potential audience upwards of 100,000. Pastor Ulrich Parzany had invited me to participate in an interview during the pre-programme session on the last evening.

So much for planning. My family recalls that time with absolute horror. It began when our dog, Blacky, began coughing strangely. I'm not sure "coughing" is an accurate term for the horrible noise coming from his throat. A few days later, he was unable to walk straight, and his muscle coordination difficulties quickly progressed to an inability to swallow. He couldn't even get his own saliva down, so began foaming at the mouth. Blacky became aggressive, biting our son Florian's hand twice and lunging at me, spraying saliva in the process. We came to the devastating conclusion that our beloved dog had contracted rabies.

I sat in my office, watching as Florian knelt by Blacky, sobbing. It nearly broke my heart, and Tina's too. We knew Blacky could not survive. As if this weren't awful enough, we had to consider the possibility that any one of us might have become infected ourselves. While there is a slim chance of surviving a disease such as Ebola, once symptoms of rabies manifest in an organism, including humans, there is virtually no chance of recovery. It is a death sentence. The World Health Organization estimates that 50,000 people die from this virus each year in a most painful and wretched manner.

On Friday 1 March, I was due to fly to Mexico in order to deliver two presentations in the city of Toluca. I was standing on our veranda, looking out into the garden, when I saw something so alarming that shivers ran down my spine. Our dog Blacky was jumping backwards, all across the garden, in clear agony. I have never seen anything like that before, nor could I fathom how a dog's anatomy could actually facilitate such a bizarre movement. My wife and I knew we had no choice but to put Blacky out of his misery. We put him down by means of an injection directly into his heart. It was terrible for all of us.

The rabies virus causes physical changes in an infected organism's brain. If a pathologist finds that Negri bodies have developed within the nerve cells, it is a red alert for any human who has had contact with the animal. They must be vaccinated immediately, and if the person has been bitten, injections must be given around the bite as soon as possible to improve the chances of survival. This is known as post-exposure prophylaxis, or PEP.

An hour before we put Blacky down, Florian, Martina and I had started a vaccination series. We had only received one dose at that point. There were five more to follow.

GOD HAS SEEN US

At about 10 a.m. I was in a taxi, headed to the airport so I could fly to Mexico. I was exhausted before I'd even started. At the same time, staff were taking our dog's corpse to the pathology department in Abancay for testing. My son left for school, broken-hearted. My wife went to work at the hospital.

Late Saturday morning, Mexican doctor Daniel Fuentes picked me up from the airport in Mexico City. My presentation was to take place that evening at the General Lopez Mateo Hospital. I had physically made it to Mexico, but my mind and heart were miles away. Rabies. I could not stop thinking about Florian. The bites on his hand were ten days old. That was a long time when talking about rabies. Could the virus have reached his brain by now?

I got through my presentation, and I sat at my computer in the hotel. I was miserable. I Googled recommended strategies for preventing the contraction of rabies. My wife was back in Curahuasi doing the exact same thing. I phoned her, and we decided that Florian most definitely needed to receive the PEP injections around the wound – but where could he get these?

Tina made phone calls all over the world, and I sought information from the hospitals in Lima. Incredibly, not a single hospital in this city of 8 million people had the vaccination Florian needed. I was told that only the US embassy had a small supply of the rabies antibodies, kept chilled in a refrigerator, but it was only for American use.

By midnight, we had made a decision. Tina would fly with Florian from Cusco to Lima, and then on to Quito, Ecuador. Mission doctor Eckehart Wolff, whom we had been able to reach via mobile, assured us that the vaccination needed was available at a nearby hospital. Dr Wolff himself administered the PEP, and my family was home within twenty-four hours.

My stay in Mexico was over and I was waiting in Orlando for my connecting flight to Frankfurt. I Skyped Tina to ask if she had heard anything from the pathology department in Abancay, where we had sent Blacky's body.

"Yes, it's rabies. The lab confirmed it."

I was devastated. Every day the mass media exposes us to seemingly endless stories of great suffering. And yet somehow we can still sleep at night because we are not personally affected. But when it hits your world, your family, via a devastating illness or tragic accident.... Perhaps you can then understand why Christians put their hope in God's promise to one day wipe away all our tears. There shall be no mourning, nor crying, nor pain in a place the Bible calls heaven.

In the end, the rabies diagnosis turned out to be wrong, thank God. Our dog must have had distemper instead, which has similar symptoms but is not harmful to humans. There are no words to express our relief at this revelation.

On 5 March, I picked up my rental car at Frankfurt airport. On 7 March, I gave my first presentation of the tour, in Freudenberg near Siegen. I hoped that the 140 people present in that Protestant church hall were able to focus on the presentation and were not too distracted by the fact that I was clearly coming down with something. I coughed into the microphone and blew my nose so often my tissues were soaked. I suppose it was all to be expected after such a week of incredible stress – the fear, the lack of sleep, the jetlag, and the travel itself had now come together for revenge on my body. It was now Thursday, and in three days I was due on stage at the ProChrist event to share the story of Diospi Suyana – with a fever, swollen lips, and virtually no voice.

I have been praying to God for many years. I don't ask Him for an easy life, but I do ask to feel His presence. He always comes through. With the frequent separation from my family, the massive responsibility for the work, and "unplanned excitement"/little emergencies of one kind or another, my life really is not easy. There are days when I sit in the corner of some airport and feel close to defeat. But God gives me and my family signs of His presence and peace, and it all becomes worth it once again.

After the Freudenberg presentation, I drove back to Wiesbaden, feeling as though the flu virus was taking over my entire body. I felt so discouraged and appealed to God to make me well again. I so wanted to have the energy and enthusiasm in Stuttgart to share stories of His great faithfulness. I didn't want to look as pathetic as I currently felt. I had been praying for this ProChrist opportunity for months. It had the potential to be so powerful, encouraging Christians in their faith and challenging atheists to re-examine their beliefs. And now this! The previous two weeks had wreaked havoc on my body.

The next morning, I woke up feeling better than I had for ages. It took me a minute to fully realize that my illness was *gone*. No more runny nose. No more sore throat or cough. No more exhaustion and aching joints. All had completely disappeared!

On Sunday evening, I stood on the stage in Stuttgart, relaxed and feeling well. As I answered the questions posed by presenter Jürgen Werth, I think it is safe to say that the audience "caught the spark". A hundred thousand people that day heard the miraculous story of Diospi Suyana, a hospital created and maintained by faith. Following my interview, Christians from 800 Catholic and Protestant churches responded generously

GOD HAS SEEN US

through financial offerings shared among four charitable projects. One of these projects was Diospi Suyana.

On 28 May, Olaf Böttger, chairman of Diospi Suyana, flew to Berlin for a ceremony during which the gifts were presented, along with other donations. Volker Kauder, a German politician, also attended the ceremony.

Christians had given more than €100,000 in response to my interview, an amount equivalent to $140,000 at the current exchange rate. This meant we had the lion's share of the cost of a new CT scanner in hand! We received more support from the Christian Medical Aid Association, which had dissolved the previous summer and donated its remaining funds of €40,000, or $54,000, to Diospi Suyana for the express purpose of purchasing a CT scanner.

Months later, I sat in the executive office at Tecnasa, an IT solutions company located in the southern part of Lima. Both director Jorge del Busto and his son Andres had been familiar with Diospi Suyana for years. Now was the time for them to make their contribution to the cause. Instead of doubling the import fees, standard practice in Peru, Tecnasa agreed to forgo any profit. Under these conditions, I was very happy to sign the contract for a brand new scanner made by Hitachi. The price of this state-of-the-art machine in Japan is approximately €160,000, or $215,000, so it was within our budget.

We gained our needed CT machine not because the president of Siemens Healthcare had changed his mind, but because Europeans and Peruvians, Catholics and Protestants, had all come together as the hands and feet of Christ.

GOD HAS SEEN US

12

The Battle for Container 32

Back when we were students, and even before that, my wife and I were involved with all kinds of interesting social activist movements. In addition to being involved with various ministries at our church, we occasionally linked arms with other kindred spirits around American missile bases. We also protested the construction of the western runway at Frankfurt airport because of the 3 million trees that would be destroyed in the process.

I have no idea whether or not our participation in these events actually made a difference to the causes we were supporting, but it did sharpen our social conscience. I showed up at the doors of Amnesty International. I wrote indignant letters to foreign dictators, demanding the release of political prisoners. Naturally, even the most heinous of villains is reduced to trembling once their letter box and email overflow with angry missives!

Over the years, I have always held the possibility of a collective post or email campaign at the back of my mind, knowing that the day could come when we would need to exercise the option on behalf of Diospi Suyana.

It was a hot Tuesday, 22 June 2012. I switched the car air conditioning to full blast as I followed the satnav to Bad Bocklet for an early-afternoon meeting with Frau Roer. Frau Roer was a spirited entrepreneur who several years earlier had founded DT&SHOP, a special mail order company for dental laboratory supplies. The large, brightly lit facility that housed her company exuded a sense of innovation, both inside and out.

Several minutes after my arrival, we were sitting together in a conference room. The attractive executive attentively viewed the pictures of Diospi Suyana as they appeared on the screen. As soon as I had finished my presentation, Frau Roer wasted no time in sharing her opinion.

"Dr John, religious faith has been the cause of a great deal of harm throughout history." She had obviously seen through to the essence of our work: faith in God. "I personally am a feminist, and during a visit to India I was able to broaden my horizons greatly," she continued. "Diospi Suyana is simply too narrow-minded for my taste."

I felt suddenly discouraged. I did not know how best to reply, so I said nothing. Frau Roer let her criticism of our mission work fly freely, and I feared that my hours spent driving here had been nothing more than wasted time. Mentally, I was already packing my bag.

"But of course we want to help you."

What did she just say?

"Send us a list of the things you need for the lab."

Why she changed gear and made that offer, I will never know. Upon Frau Roer's instruction, DT&SHOP donated an entire year's worth of dental supplies to our lab. All the products were top quality and carefully packed – a very generous six-figure donation.

On Christmas Day 2012, the dockworkers in Lima/Callao unloaded container 32 from the ship and transported it to the DP World container depot. The contents of the container included the precious supplies from DT&SHOP. Our customs agent, Monte Sion, contacted the state authorities for information regarding the payment of customs duties on freight. Letters and emails were exchanged, and phone calls made, but somehow there was a spanner thrown in the works.

Early in the morning of Friday 4 January, the depot workers unloaded all 218 crates from the container. An official from the General Directorate of Infrastructure Equipment and Maintenance of the Ministry of Health (DGEIM) was supposed to come and inspect the contents, but he didn't show up. Mr Sion made calls in the afternoon to remind them, but to no avail. In the end, our donated goods, valued at $202,000, were returned to the container. It reminded me of the *Hornberger Schießen*, or Hornberger Shooting. This German idiom refers to an event that is expected to be spectacular but then fizzles out to great disappointment. There was no use getting upset about it. In fact, the disinterested workers ended up having to load and unload our crates a total of five times before this was over.

My telephone call to the staff at DGEIM was not particularly friendly. At my behest, a "crisis management" meeting was held at the DGEIM offices that evening, during which I shared the Diospi Suyana story from my laptop.

"I wasn't aware of the significance of Diospi Suyana," one of the officials said. "I'll have the paperwork filled out first thing tomorrow morning."

As the meeting came to a close, it appeared that the darkness surrounding our container was beginning to lift.

Between 2003 and 2013, I had done battle with the authorities in Lima and Apurímac on many occasions, and had long since learned that the Peruvian government places the most ridiculous stumbling blocks in the way of aid to its people.

Days went by with no progress. The fees for storing the container in the depot, as well as the costs incurred through CMA, the French transportation company, multiplied exponentially, and I realized I would need to redouble my efforts in order to get the container released.

With the help of several politicians, I was granted an audience with the Deputy Minister of Health, Dr José Carlos del Carmen. The Deputy Minister and his staff listened attentively as I relayed the grievous saga of a benevolent mission besieged by government bureaucracy.

Dr José Carlos del Carmen responded succinctly: "That container needs to be through Customs *tomorrow*!"

I thanked him for his good intentions. Unfortunately, they made no difference whatsoever. The container did not budge.

On Tuesday 22 January, I called the director of DIGEMID, Peru's medical device market regulator. Señor Pedro Luis Yarasca had never heard of Diospi Suyana, but his officials had removed all the DT&SHOP supplies from the container on the outrageous premise that they had no use-by date. I had, however, been informed by DT&SHOP that they did not require a use-by date as they were not perishable. DIGEMID had simply taken $40,000 worth of supplies. The tone of our conversation intensified. The director clearly had no compassion for our patients or hospital – that much was evident. Nor was he swayed by any of my arguments. This indifference in government officials irritates me no end.

"Señor Yarasca," I finally yelled into the telephone receiver, "if you won't help me, I will go to the people of Peru!"

My warning did not faze Señor Yarasca. He responded coldly, "Go right ahead. I have no problem with that."

My efforts at diplomacy through email and telephone continued persistently over 23 and 24 January, but I was getting nowhere. Nowhere.

That evening I sat at my desk and wracked my brain for a solution. Thirty days had passed since the container had arrived in the country. Diospi Suyana was attempting to bring in more than $200,000 worth of supplies for the good of the Peruvian people who needed it most, and yet the authorities were responding with callous disinterest. Even my meeting with the Deputy Minister of Health had yielded not one step forward.

I recalled my letters to Amnesty International thirty years previously. What if I were to use the Diospi Suyana website to make our predicament public? I could beseech friends from all over the world to engage in an extensive email campaign, putting pressure on the authorities blocking the release of critical supplies. Of course, there was risk. I would not only be standing up to corruption but also directly challenging it. As the saying goes, "You can't beat the system." But if God would extend His blessing to our pursuit, we would succeed.

Late into the night, I wrote a news article with the heading "SOS – Your Help is Needed Immediately!" I described our predicament and urged supporters to send brief but courteous emails requesting the release of our donated supplies. The emails were to be sent to four recipients: the Minister of Health, Señora Midori de Habich; the Deputy Minister of Health, Dr José Carlos del Carmen; the Chair of the Congressional Committee on Health, Señora Karla Schaefer; and the director of DIGEMID, Señor Pedro Luis

Yarasca. I requested that Diospi Suyana be copied in on all the emails.

The next step was to inform press representatives and other key people who I hoped would have my back. At midnight, Peruvian time, the first emails started rolling in. I stayed up several more hours, growing increasingly hopeful as my inbox filled.

Was I afraid? Absolutely. I felt I had just taken on a giant, and I had no idea how this day would end. But just like David facing Goliath, I prayed – full of uncertainty and apprehension, yet assured that God would intervene. This wasn't for me. It was for the poor patients victimized by the heartless bureaucrats.

On Saturday 26 January I thanked Diospi Suyana friends from all over the world. Within just twenty-four hours, more than 2,000 emails had been sent as requested to the recipients I had named. Messages had been sent from Germany, Switzerland, Austria, Belgium, the Netherlands, Great Britain, Finland, Romania, Sweden, Ecuador, Chile, Peru, Singapore, Japan, Tonga, South Africa, Canada, and the USA. When those government officials powered up their computers on Monday morning, they would be hit with a deluge demanding action, and a decision of one kind or another would be made.

I now needed to travel to Lima to pursue this objective in person. At the beginning of the week, I sought backing from the media. *El Comercio*, Peru's largest newspaper, published a disparaging article. *La Republica*, a tabloid, printed my original email to the Minister of Health, word for word. Renato Canales, press chief for Channel 5, supported me by broadcasting an interview during the midday and evening news.

I sought assistance from the German embassy. Upon the ambassador's direction, diplomats regularly phoned the Ministry of Health for progress updates. Container 32 was now an internationally known scandal. Christians of all denominations put their hands together in prayer for divine intervention.

Weeks later, a congressman told me of a conversation he had had with the Minister of Health during our email "assault".

"I get thousands of emails every day, and whenever I turn on my laptop, there are more. What shall I do?" Señora Midori de Habich had complained.

"Release the container," the congressman advised, "otherwise you'll get thousands more!"

On the morning of Wednesday 30 January, I sat opposite Señor Yarasca in his office at DIGEMID. The tension between us was nearly palpable.

I unpacked my laptop, and with grim determination told him the story of Diospi Suyana. A week earlier, he had been unmoved when I had told him I would appeal to the people of Peru. Then, to his great consternation, the people had responded – via TV, print media, and thousands of emails from at least twenty countries. People from Europe, Asia, Africa, and the Americas had exhorted him to act on behalf of the Quechua people in the Peruvian highlands.

Whether Señor Yarasca was touched by our story, he gave no indication. He simply stated, "We released your container this morning."

That was it. The fight was over and we had won!

I dashed out of the building in my excitement to share our victory. As soon as I found a table in a nearby restaurant,

I jumped online to share the miraculous news on our website. Messages of congratulations and praise to the God who had made this happen began to pour in.

I think this story is unique in the history of Peru. Non-governmental organizations usually back down if their goods get stuck in Customs. Vast amounts of humanitarian and medical aid never reach the intended recipients, and the poor continue to suffer.

Not everyone agreed with the way I handled this situation. We received three critical responses. A lecturer at the seminary in Lima suggested that I had caused long-term damage to the evangelical movement in Peru. He predicted political ramifications, since it is not possible to "beat the system" – at least not with impunity.

I disagreed.

A year and a half later, in June 2014, I had the opportunity to share the Diospi Suyana story with the Minister of Health. Despite the aggressive email campaign, which could not have been forgotten, she invited me to her office and listened attentively.

When I was finished, Señora de Habich smiled at me graciously. "Dr John, do not worry about the challenges. You are a man of faith."

And with that she shook my hand and was off to her next engagement.

13

The Perfect Media Event

I nformation about Diospi Suyana is readily available to anyone who wants to know more about our Christian work. We are completely transparent in everything we do, and are always open to sharing with those who wish to learn more. There are no secrets, no skeletons to come crashing unexpectedly out of our closets.

Of course, this level of openness invites criticism. For some, we are too religious. For others, not religious enough. There are those who denounce our inclusive approach to the Catholic Church, and those who feel we are not inclusive enough. I hear a subtle reproach that the quality of treatment provided by Diospi Suyana is too good for the people who receive it. Sadly, people exist who truly believe that expired medication and obsolete equipment are completely acceptable for the poor in this world.

The bottom line is that anyone who comes to visit us in Curahuasi will find things exactly as they have seen in our presentations and read in our reports, without pretence.

The very first newspaper article about Diospi Suyana appeared in our home town of Wiesbaden at the end of December 2003. By spring of 2019 our story had been covered more than 500 times in various media formats. The initial count represents print media coverage in specific geographic areas, but once an in-depth documentary was featured on Deutsche Welle TV, "at the heart of Europe", and broadcast worldwide, there was no reason nor means to continue a precise tally. In October 2014, Bethel TV shared a similar feature with Africa and the Arabian Peninsula.

Adding up the projected number of viewers through TV ratings, the circulation rates of various print media, and the hits on our website, it is safe to estimate that between 50 and 100 million people have now heard of Diospi Suyana.

In our own country, Germany, I was particularly pleased with the article that appeared on Easter Sunday 2011 in *Sonntag Aktuell*, a conglomeration of forty-six secular news sources, with an estimated 2 million readers. On page 2, an extensive article about the "Hospital of Hope" highlighted the faith basis of our work without apology. In fact, with honour.

Unfortunately, some journalists try to write God out of the Diospi Suyana story and present it as merely "a doctor's dream". My wife had the opportunity to be interviewed in Munich on Bayern 2's *Eins zu Eins* show. Her interview actually followed that of the former German president, Roman Herzog. The show host asked my wife where she got the strength to do her work. Martina replied that she read her Bible and prayed every morning. When the interview was broadcast five days later, her answer had been edited out. This is not responsible journalism; it is censorship. Fortunately, events like this are the exception rather than the rule.

In our adoptive country of Peru, there have been forty-one television reports about Diospi Suyana, in addition to radio broadcasts and print articles. The reporters and camera-crew members have become our best friends. When times get tough, I can always ask them to cast the spotlight in our direction, both literally and figuratively. I do my best to make sure Diospi Suyana is covered in the national media at least once a year.

Peru's most widely circulated weekly magazine, *SOMOS*, wrote about Diospi Suyana in an article entitled "Angels of the Andes" back in September 2006. At that point, there was only a construction site on the outskirts of Curahuasi, which looked nothing like the modern hospital it is today. From 2008, I kept an eye out for an appropriate opportunity to present the "finished product" for a follow-up story.

On 6 July 2012 we held a formal ceremony in our hospital chapel. With reporters and television crews present, Adriana Rubio, Director General of Roche in Peru, presented the hospital with three pieces of laboratory equipment valued together at approximately $100,000. The night before the big event, my wife and our daughter Natalie had traced the silhouette of each piece of donated equipment so accurately that their artwork looked deceptively like the real thing. We all smiled at their clever trick.

Naturally interested in publicity for their generous donation, the Roche PR department had invited a team of journalists from *SOMOS* to Curahuasi.

The media are not always easy to work with. Some of them are notoriously unreliable. They phone, wanting to start immediately, then cancel at the last minute – repeatedly. Sometimes the whole story just gets shelved and forgotten.

Over the next several months, the Roche PR team and I were in touch frequently, but we never saw *SOMOS*. There was always something else going on, some reason for them to cancel. Unfortunately, I did not have the contact details for the journalists, or I would have followed them up myself.

On 29 November 2012, mine owner Guido del Castillo formally presented the Spanish version of my book in his very own museum in Lima. Among the eighty guests sat Pilar Nores, the former First Lady of Peru. In order to be able to share an informed opinion, she had thoroughly read all 270 pages. Although Peru is not generally known as a nation of readers, approximately forty bookshops had opted to stock my book.

In the days leading up to this event, I had reached out to a number of reporters, inviting them to attend. Journalist Renzo Guerrero, from the daily *El Comercio*, had promised to be there. As he accepted my invitation, he mentioned that he would be bringing a colleague from *SOMOS*, Gabriela Machuca, who had expressed interest in Diospi Suyana. At last I had a *SOMOS* contact!

On 18 January I dropped by the *SOMOS* main office. Next to me at the table sat Gabriela Machuca, who had somehow managed to make time for me despite her very full schedule. I began to whip through the presentation on my computer as fast as I could. Just as I was getting going, Señora Machuca stopped me.

"I see that we need to come to Curahuasi. You have more than convinced me!" she declared.

So on 31 January Señora Machuca arrived at the hospital with a photographer, Lucero del Castillo. The plan was to begin work the next morning.

And what happened on 1 February? The 100,000th patient crossed the threshold of the hospital! None of us could have possibly orchestrated that incredible coincidence. It was a media event made in heaven.

Hermelinda Contreras, a shy farmer's wife from the mountains, must have felt it was all a dream. She had certainly never before encountered the attention and star treatment she received that day. In the waiting room, we asked for everyone's attention. Tina and I extended our heartfelt congratulations, and Stefan Seiler, our hospital administrator, presented her with a huge gift basket. The attached gift voucher indicated that all diagnostic tests and treatment would be covered by the hospital.

So what was troubling Señora Contreras that fine day? A sore throat or upset stomach? Or maybe she had just come to us out of curiosity? We never could have imagined what had brought her through our doors.

The poor Quechua woman had travelled for two full days in the hope of finding some relief. She was no stranger to pain – her husband had taken an axe to her skull years before during a drunken rage. But that wound had long since healed. Today her problem was neurocysticercosis, a disease in which the larvae of the pork tapeworm penetrate the wall of the colon and form fluid-filled cysts in internal organs, causing calcification. If the brain is affected, the patient will experience severe headaches and seizures.

As Señora Contreras was positioned in the CT scanner, Gabriela and Lucero were at her side. They could not have wished for a better hook for their report on Diospi Suyana than the chronicle of this woman's experience.

On 15 February Gabriela Muchuca got back in touch to follow up: "Dear Dr John, I am writing with the good news that the article will be published tomorrow with a five-page spread.… It is of course impossible to tell the entire incredible story of Diospi Suyana in such a space, but I have done what I can. I hope the report will help you win political support and touch hearts."

Five full pages in *SOMOS* is as extraordinary as five pages in the *Stern* magazine in Germany or *The Economist* in Britain!

The first double-page spread depicted Señora Contreras lying in the scanner, with radiographer John Lentik and nurse Silvia Escalantes peering in from one end. The headline boldly declared Diospi Suyana to be "The Hospital of Faith". The journalists described in detail how they met our 100,000th patient and observed her treatment at our hands.

There are people in the West who believe religion is boring; that faith is something for tired old ladies. Why fall asleep in a church service when you can be stimulated by watching a Formula 1 race on TV? Adventure and God are perceived as being diametrically opposed. I personally could not disagree more. It has been my experience that when we put our faith in God and allow Him to use us as His hands and feet here on earth – that is when the excitement really starts.

We struggle to save our patients' lives only to receive a court summons for our efforts. Out of the blue, an ugly, inflammatory email is spread widely. I often find myself groaning with frustration, even questioning God as to why such experiences must be endured.

But then we gain a lift for our hospital as a result of a casual dinner. And we have journalists from a major publication present just as the 100,000th patient arrives for treatment at Diospi Suyana….

God is not dull. He is the most creative author in all eternity. His stories have unexpected twists and turns, loads of suspense, plenty of action, and impeccable timing.

His stories are our lives.

14

Where Does it Hurt?

Neurocysticercosis. A brain full of cysts caused by a pork tapeworm. The very idea is enough to turn your stomach.

I am often asked, "What diseases do the Quechua typically suffer from?"

My standard answer is "The same as you – plus the diseases caused by poverty."

This wretched combination of poverty, indifference, and superstition is responsible for so many human tragedies in developing countries. Based on its Gross Domestic Product (GDP), Peru is not actually a "Third World" country. The white population is doing well, and even people of mixed race generally have enough to survive. But the indigenous people in the Andes live forgotten and despised, in conditions as desperate as any my wife and I observed in West Africa. The tragic companion of poverty is very often social injustice. There are so many stories I could share regarding the appalling realities of daily life for the Quechua.

One indigenous woman and her thirteen-year-old son Jorge had travelled six hours by bus from their home to the Diospi Suyana hospital. The mother was very concerned – her son simply was not growing. Something had to be horribly wrong. My wife's diagnosis of the boy was confirmed by our lab: he had a hereditary thyroid deficiency. Since there are no newborn screenings in the Andes, his hormone deficiency had been neither detected nor treated. Jorge stood at just under a metre in height – about as tall as a typical three-year-old. His resulting cognitive impairment would limit his future employment and independent living prospects. It need not have been this way. Had Jorge received hormone treatment earlier, he would have been able to develop quite normally.

Every year thousands of tourists visit Peru. Some develop a fascination with the traditional remedies of the curanderos (healers). They often ask whether I would be willing to work with them. There is much to be learned from the thousands of years that natural medicine has been practised, but the question brings to mind Rodrigo Huaman, a man from Curahuasi who had been drinking far too much for years. A wide variety of alcoholic beverages, including his own home-made moonshine, had wreaked havoc on his brain, and he often suffered from seizures. His family took him to a curandero. Curanderos sometimes exploit the widespread belief in and fear of spirits, charging exorbitant fees and insisting on up-front cash payment.

Rodrigo was already unconscious when the curandero began his healing ritual. He poured a potion into the man's mouth but, in his unconscious state, Rodrigo was unable to cough, so some of the liquid flowed directly into his lungs. The contents of the potion caused dangerously high acid levels in Rodrigo's blood.

By the time Rodrigo was brought to Diospi Suyana, he was seizing every ten minutes. Dr Washburn and his team did everything they could to help the man as his life hung by a thread. Thankfully, in the end, Rodrigo survived.

There really is no simple cure for alcoholism or superstition. Many of our patients seek to survive rather than truly live. The Quechua people suffer more than most.

At the beginning of October 2014, a doctor from Cusco contacted us to see if Dr Buck, our eye specialist, could conduct an exam under anaesthesia for a small boy whose older brother had accidentally pierced his eye with a wooden stick. There were fears of serious damage.

Our staff waited for the child and his family all day. They didn't come. Nor did they come the next day. Finally, on that Friday evening, the mother led the boy in, holding his hand. She carried a baby on her back. We learned that the family simply had no money for the journey. Two full days had passed before they had been able to borrow the money from friends and neighbours. On the way to Curahuasi, the boy's father learned that his only cow had escaped the care of the other children remaining at home. He turned back to search for it.

At the clinic, the mother was distraught, fearing she would not have enough money for the treatment to save her son's eye. Dr Buck was able to calm her as the child was admitted to the ward. The boy's eye was so swollen, the operation had to be postponed. Three days later, a microscopic examination of the eye revealed a torn sclera and a ruptured choroid. Dr Buck carefully removed the splinter that remained in the wound, then sutured the cut. Follow-up examinations showed that this treatment had saved the boy's vision. The Quechua family paid a token fee of 20 soles, or approximately $7. The remaining costs of the surgery and treatment were covered by donations.

The Andes mountains are beautiful but dangerous. An elderly indigenous woman lay motionless on a stretcher, and the accompanying doctor gave us a brief summary of events.

The previous evening, seventy-eight-year-old Maria Barazorda had been working out in some terraced fields. Farming this terrain is extremely difficult; each step must be made carefully to ensure placement on level ground. This can be particularly challenging in the fading light of dusk. Maria lost her footing and tumbled several metres down the slope. Pain shot through her back and left hip. She tried to get up but couldn't. Everything hurt. The last rays of the setting sun disappeared over the distant snow-capped mountains. Soon the night wrapped the mountains and valley in a shroud of darkness.

Nobody heard Maria shout for help. Nobody knew where she was. As she lay uncomfortably on a bed of thorns and stones, the temperature began to drop. As the hours passed, Maria didn't know if she would survive the night or freeze to death.

Miraculously, Maria made it through the night. Her relatives found her in the emerging grey of dawn. The X-rays showed no broken bones. At Diospi Suyana, she received warmth, care, and painkillers – and made a full recovery.

No two days at Diospi Suyana are alike, and it seems every week brings something new and unexpected. For many years now, I have posted daily updates on the Diospi Suyana website, enabling our readers to participate in our "adventures". On 27 October 2010, I shared the details of an incredible day.

> *It is a Wednesday morning. As I get out of the car*
> *at the hospital, I notice a large bus at the door. I*

*learn that two Australians and an American have
arrived with fourteen patients from Cusco. After
morning devotions, the usual madness commences
throughout the hospital. An indigenous woman
complains to me that she cannot get a ticket,
therefore she cannot get an appointment. Together
we approach Evarista Carraso, who is in charge
of distributing the tickets. She states that there are
currently thirty people on the waiting list for today,
and the doctors are fully booked for Thursday and
Friday as well.*

*In operating theatre #1, Dr Jens Hassfeld
struggles with a large placenta that has found
its way into a patient's abdomen. It is not where
it is supposed to be, and Dr Hassfeld needs to
remove it. The amount of blood would have
caused most observers to faint, but Dr Hassfeld
is standing strong. The patient will be very
grateful to him later.*

*At 10 a.m. officials from Lima arrive to
inspect our blood bank. First, I tell them the
story of Diospi Suyana and offer them a tour of
the entire hospital. Three hours later, we arrive
at the blood bank. By now, our visitors from
Lima are in awe of Diospi Suyana and voicing
the desire for other hospitals to function as we
do.*

*At midday, I learn of three patients
requiring emergency surgery. Dr Hassfeld
somehow finds the strength to remove a twisted
ovarian cyst. Julia Noeske, a new paediatrician
from Germany, is supposed to be spending her
first afternoon with us examining children, but*

GOD HAS SEEN US

instead finds herself very capably assisting in
the operating theatre.

Medical technician Tobias Lächele is
taking the English-speaking visitors from the
bus on a guided tour of the hospital. Like
everyone else who comes to Diospi Suyana, the
women cannot contain their surprise at the high
standard of care available here.

Surgeon Matthias Stephan is now removing
a festering appendix. It's Jens Hassfeld's
turn once again as a young woman's life is
jeopardized by an ectopic pregnancy.

The Australians have expressed their
gratitude and taken their leave. The inspectors
have also now departed for Abancay. The
patients in intensive care lie recovering on
their beds. The exhausted doctors and nurses
head home for some rest. During the night I
will set out again to exchange friendly words
with officials in the capital. So much could
happen before three in the morning. But is there
anywhere else our staff would want to be than
here at Diospi Suyana? I doubt it!

Diospi Suyana is not only a hospital built to serve the needs of the poor; it is also a mission hospital. Its uniquely Christian focus sometimes hits a nerve. I had just finished a presentation at Leipzig University, when a female student challenged, "A hospital is a great idea, but why does it have to be a mission hospital?"

Whenever such objections are raised, I respond by sharing this story: It had been a long, exhausting day. Dr Luz

GOD HAS SEEN US

Peña and my wife Martina were nearly finished, with just one more patient waiting to be seen. It was a complicated case. The young man had presented with a tumour eating into his chest.

"We do not have the treatment you need here," my wife said. "You need to go to the Instituto Nacional de Enfermedades Neoplásicas, the large cancer hospital in Lima. Perhaps the doctors there can help you."

The patient shook his head. "I've already been there. They are the ones who referred me to you!"

Martina knew that the man had made the twenty-hour bus trip to Curahuasi for a reason. "Just a moment," she said. "I'll be right back."

A few minutes later, the dying man was given a booklet about the Christian faith and a copy of the Diospi Suyana story. There they all stood in the waiting room: two doctors, the man whose life was being cut short, and his family. The doctors wasted no time.

"You know, when I go home tonight, a car could hit me as I cross the highway. If that happens, what happens to me? Where do I go when I die?"

The atmosphere in the waiting room suddenly seemed to be charged with electricity.

"I know where I am going," my wife continued. "Because Jesus died on the cross for my sins, heaven is waiting for me. Would you like to go there too?" Martina bent over the patient and slowly formulated a prayer that the dying man could repeat after her, phrase by phrase, consciously placing his life into the hands of a God he had not known.

Tears ran down every face. The man was crying, his wife and brother too. Even the doctors wiped their eyes. These were not tears of despair or pity. In the midst of this otherwise empty waiting room, all five felt the presence of a holy and living God.

When asked how I deal with the mission aspect, my answer is "positively". We cannot see any viable alternative to faith in Jesus Christ. Not in Peru, nor anywhere else in the world.

15

The Opportunist

The taxi dropped me at my front door just before lunchtime on Monday 2 April 2012. I had just returned from a two-week whirlwind trip through Germany and Austria, into which I had crammed sixteen presentations. The next day, I had my colleagues brief me on all that had occurred during my absence.

"Klaus, you must examine this Señora Quispe – it's urgent!" my wife Tina said. "A visiting surgeon removed her gall bladder three weeks ago, and her latest ultrasound shows quite a lot of fluid in her abdomen. I am very concerned."

The years 2011 and 2012 were not easy ones for Diospi Suyana. We got the basics accomplished with short-term volunteer surgeons, not all of whom spoke decent Spanish. As they stayed with us only a short time – just a few weeks – follow-up care was somewhat lacking in continuity.

I studied the patient's case notes. The laparoscopic removal of the gall bladder had been an unremarkable, routine procedure. On the day following her operation, the surgeon noted his satisfaction at her progress. He got on a plane to return to Germany, and she got on a bus for a ten-hour ride to her home in Puno. Now she was back.

I gently pressed on Señora Quispe's abdomen. She winced in pain as I moved my hands to her right side. She was not at all well – even a medical novice would have recognized that. One needed only to look at her face to see how poorly she was.

I explained my "battle plan" to Señora Quispe and her husband. "It looks like bile is leaking from the gall bladder base," I said, regretfully. "I recommend we rinse out the abdominal cavity and insert a tube for drainage. Bile leaks usually dry up on their own."

My suspicions were confirmed at the first incision: the excess fluid was indeed bile. I rinsed the abdominal cavity with saline, then inserted a drainage tube under her liver.

In the days following the surgery, Señora Quispe seemed to be recovering reasonably well. She was able to walk around and had an appetite to eat her meals. Her blood pressure, pulse, and temperature were all within normal limits.

But then, quite suddenly, Señora Quispe's condition deteriorated rapidly. The ultrasound again revealed a massive accumulation of fluid. I had a keen sense of foreboding.

Señora Quispe was returned to the operating theatre. I had to open her up yet again in order to determine what was causing the problem. Through a long incision across her abdomen, it did not take long to identify the source of her trouble. When removing her gall bladder, the team of surgeons had accidentally nicked the bile duct. This can normally be ameliorated by inserting a T tube for drainage as the wound heals. To my horror, I saw that the duct was sliced all the way up to the liver, leaving me no tissue with which to perform corrective surgery.

My surgical assistant and I tried everything we could think of. We attempted to close the bile duct, but found it to be a hopeless task. My mouth went dry as I failed to correct this gall bladder surgery gone horribly wrong. I packed the abdominal cavity with compresses to stave the bleeding and closed the incision I had made.

"We need to transfer her to Lima," I said with frustration. "Maybe an expert liver surgeon can create a bypass to the small intestine."

In emergencies, the Diospi Suyana team is unbelievably fast. Within half an hour the ambulance was en route to Cusco, with Dr Hassfeld and me accompanying the patient. From Cusco, we would continue on to Lima via air. I utilized my contacts with the Clinica Angloamericana, sharing the operation details with the best liver surgeon in Peru, Dr Franco, and requesting his assistance.

"I will see what I can do," the Peruvian doctor promised.

Señora Quispe survived the transfer to Lima, and after a few diagnostic tests she was taken into surgery for the third time in just ten days. I phoned regularly to check on her progress, but the news was grim. The surgeon was fighting for her with all he had. In such critical moments, time seems to stop, and waiting goes on for an eternity.

Finally, after eight long hours, the operation was over. Dr Franco had managed to attach a loop from the small intestine to the bile duct. This extremely delicate and painstaking procedure was started in the afternoon and lasted long into the night.

Just before midnight Dr Franco called me with the outcome: "Dr John, I have managed the best I could, but I cannot promise the sutures will hold in such inflamed tissue."

Day after day, missionaries in Curahuasi were putting their hands together in prayer for God's blessing on Señora Quispe. The sutures did in fact hold, but it took many weeks for her to fully recover.

The Clinica Angloamericana is not a mission hospital. In contrast, it is actually one of the most expensive medical facilities in Peru. While Dr Franco graciously declined payment for his services, the remaining medical fees came to approximately $20,000. A large sum, but perhaps not so much when it pays to save the life of a mother of four.

About ten days later, Señor Quispe appeared in my office. He wasted no time in demanding that Diospi Suyana pay the outstanding balance to the Clinica Angloamericana, as the bile duct damage occurred at our hospital.

"Señor Quispe," I replied, "I am very sorry that your wife went through such difficulties. An injury to the bile duct can happen at any hospital, and is one of the possible complications your wife was warned of prior to surgery. The surgeon who conducted the operation has removed thousands of gall bladders in his career, and there was no act of negligence. We are a mission hospital. We cannot pay bills incurred at other medical facilities."

"Dr John, you need to know that our 'padrino' works at the Supreme Court in Lima," the angry man retorted threateningly.

I knew exactly what he was implying, but tried to maintain a poker face, not letting him see how it unsettled me. A "padrino" is a wealthy and/or powerful person who advocates for and otherwise supports an individual or family in return for gifts and other tokens of respect.

"Perhaps we should meet with your padrino in Lima and see if we cannot come up with a reasonable solution."

Señor Quispe accepted my suggestion, and we set a date.

On 24 April we convened at a restaurant in downtown Lima. Señor Quispe, a relative, and the padrino were on one side of the table. Dr David Brady, the assistant director of Diospi Suyana, and I sat on the other side.

Collectively, they appeared as the cat who had just cornered a canary. Because we were foreigners, they assumed we had a great deal of money. Even if they could not force us to pay, they could tie us up in expensive legal proceedings for years. In South America, the hospital director bears full responsibility for all that occurs under the hospital's roof. It would be me, not the visiting surgeon from Germany, who would fight this thorny battle and bear the affiliated cost.

As Dr Brady prayed silently next to me, I showed Señor Quispe and his team pictures of Diospi Suyana and relayed how the hospital had come to be. I explained how we were not "rich gringos" to be "milked", but a mission hospital dependent on the miracles of God and the sacrifice of many volunteers and supporters just to function from day to day.

Everyone at the table was touched by the Diospi Suyana story.

"Dr John," the padrino began, "I have the greatest respect for what you, your wife, and all your colleagues are doing in Curahuasi. Nevertheless, there is a bill to be paid."

I had pre-emptively talked through the situation in detail with a firm of forty lawyers headed by Dr José Olaechea. After one of my presentations in Lima, he had made a blanket offer of legal counsel at no charge. That generous offer would now prove invaluable.

The lawyers had advised me that there was no legal obligation for Diospi Suyana to pay a penny. However, if the family took the story to the press, it could mean the end of our hospital. Furthermore, if Señora Quispe were to die, the matter could be taken all the way up to Congress!

I valued the counsel of the Olaechea lawyers. Just as Dr Olaechea had promised, they were not making a profit in this case. These top professionals were giving their time, honesty, and expertise in support of Diospi Suyana.

So, after two hours in the restaurant, we reached an agreement with Señor Quispe. Diospi Suyana would pay the bulk of the outstanding medical bills. The Olaechea firm would draw up an agreement to be signed by all, stating that by making this payment, Diospi Suyana would not be held liable for any future claims related to this case.

I'm sure you can guess what happened next.

After Diospi Suyana had made the agreed-upon payment, Señor Quispe contacted us again, this time demanding reimbursement for personal related costs, such as flights and hotels. He threatened to take us to court if payment was not made.

Señor Quispe was unrelenting. Caller ID on my mobile indicated calls from him early in the morning until late at night. Twice he visited the hospital in person to demand files that he intended to hand over to a legal team for detailed inspection.

There was no easy answer. A trial that lasted years and the risk of very public mud-slinging would be physically and emotionally exhausting – not to mention expensive. Both the hospital and my family would be driven to breaking point.

"Dr John," the Olaechea lawyers advised, "if you pay this man any more money, this extortion will never end. He will keep coming back until he has bled you dry!" Their warning was clear.

For months, my wife Tina desperately prayed to God for our protection. The burden of responsibility was on our shoulders. While other missionaries could conceivably pack their bags and go home in the face of such a crisis, we did not have that option. We were the founders of Diospi Suyana. We had invested our entire lives in this work of faith. And we would stay and fight for it, no matter how long it took.

Then one day Señor Quispe simply stopped calling. God alone knows why he suddenly abandoned his gold-digging scheme. In God's grace and mercy, He answered our prayers.

Ever since this nerve-wracking case, all doctors have had to sign an agreement with six terms, ranging from conscientious completion of patient files to avoidance of high-risk medical procedures. When high-risk treatment is necessary, my express permission is required.

God protected us during that summer of 2012, but I want to take all necessary precautions for the future.

16

Legal Drama

Our son Florian is toying with the idea of becoming a lawyer. I think this is extremely courageous. I have the utmost respect for the legal system, to the extent that I slink past courthouses hoping to remain unnoticed. I never drop litter on the street and am careful to never scratch a public defender's car (or anyone else's, for that matter!). I do everything within my power to avoid provoking these dispensers of justice, and hope that they will return the favour and leave me in peace as well.

Unfortunately, this is not always the case. I receive letters from the court that, even after careful rereading, are incomprehensible. There are deadlines to meet and fines to pay, and so on. Scarcely any other matter has caused me quite as many grey hairs, however, as that of Constructec, an Ecuadorian construction firm and my constant headache for six long years.

In January 2007, during the building phase of the hospital, we terminated our contract with Constructec owing to suspected misappropriation of funds we had received via donations. This quick solution, which cost Diospi Suyana a penalty of $39,000, was highly preferable to a long, drawn-out court battle.

A few days after the termination was signed, our civil engineer Udo Klemenz requested documentation regarding the taxation of Constructec's profits while under contract. Constructec had charged us $34,000 to cover their tax obligation to Peru. As a non-profit organization, we could then claim the $34,000 back from the tax authorities. After several combative emails, it was clear that Constructec had committed tax fraud. The owner of Constructec, Carlos Pullas, had pocketed that money, thus cheating Diospi Suyana, as we obviously could not claim back tax that had never actually been paid.

The solution was simple. Diospi Suyana deducted the missing $34,000 from the $39,000 termination fee. Udo Klemenz, chairman of Diospi Suyana Olaf Böttger, and I were satisfied, but Carlos Pullas was furious. This was clearly not the outcome he had planned.

In May 2008 I received a registered letter that was quite difficult to decipher. The general meaning became clear, however, as I saw my signature from the termination agreement staring up at me. Our Peruvian bookkeeper, Edgar Montalvo, explained the situation to me. Carlos Pullas had engaged Coface, an international debt collection agency, and was demanding full payment of the termination penalty fee.

Edgar Montalvo and I flew straight to Lima and explained the situation to officials at the Coface office. Of course, none of them had previously been aware of the tax-evasion component. They closed the file and apologized for the inconvenience.

In the summer of 2008, Diospi Suyana officially reported Constructec for tax fraud. It was now up to the Ministry of Revenue to institute legal proceedings. But the nightmare continued, as Constructec retaliated by filing charges against Diospi Suyana in the local court on 29 October. Multiple

GOD HAS SEEN US

hearings followed. Dr Olaechea and his team were once more willing to assist. The matter cost a great deal of time, sleep, and inner peace.

The battle raged for two and a half years, until the court in Curahuasi ruled against Diospi Suyana on 22 March 2011. We had lost. In his verdict, the judge determined that Diospi Suyana was bound to fulfil the terms of the termination agreement. It was then up to the Ministry of Revenue to pursue the tax evasion charges against Constructec in separate court proceedings.

We did what we had to do, and officially appealed the ruling in the Superior Court in Apurímac. The waiting game resumed. Several new justices had been appointed to the court. We were told our case file was at the bottom of their pile. Our case was not subject to a statute of limitations and could therefore be dragged on indefinitely. If the Superior Court reached the same verdict, Diospi Suyana would have to pay at least $50,000 (the contested $34,000, as well as legal fees and four years of accrued interest).

For two long years I brought up this situation for prayer at our weekly meetings. As the group entreated God for a positive resolution, I was reminded of a verse from Psalm 23: "He leads me in paths of righteousness for his name's sake" (ESV). We have always been solid in our claim that Diospi Suyana is a hospital of faith, a miracle built on the promises of God. Was this legal conflict any different? His name would be praised!

On 26 April 2013, we learned rather by chance that the court had issued a verdict – some time ago! Our contact in Abancay, a rather harried man named Tim, had simply forgotten to let us know. The court had considered our evidence and ruled that the judge in Curahuasi was bound to take into account the financial damage done to Diospi Suyana as a result of Constructec's tax evasion. I breathed a huge sigh of relief.

That afternoon I appeared before the judge in Curahuasi. The judge who had presided over our original case had long since moved to another town.

The judge regarded me and admonished, "You were not even present for the hearing!"

A sense of panic came over me. Obviously our contact person had also forgotten to tell us about the court date, and our absence had been indubitably noted. All our hard work over the last few years had been thrown to the wind by this grievous oversight. I prepared myself for the worst.

"But the other side's team wasn't here either," the judge continued.

I looked at her in disbelief. "What does that mean?" I asked anxiously.

"Since no counsel from either side showed up, the case was archived. It's over."

After six years of contest, Diospi had won by default. A few minutes later, I was in Udo Klemenz's office, rejoicing in God's deliverance.

In the Bible, there are many examples of God at work while His people are sleeping. That is essentially what happened here. We had no idea what was going on, and yet He was moving. Despite not knowing, despite not showing up, we had won!

17

Marching to the Beat
of a Different Drum

On 26 February 2013, as I was showing a TV crew around the hospital, I received a call from the front gate.

"A delegation from Puno has just arrived," the attendant informed me. "Perhaps you would like to come and welcome them."

I hurried to the gate to ascertain what exactly was going on. I saw twenty men and women standing around a large coach. I was informed that this was a prestigious contingent from the National University of the Altiplano in Puno. A rector, several deans, some engineers, and media representatives had just travelled ten hours from the south of Peru to speak with me.

"Dr John, we would like to build a hospital just like this one," the rector solemnly declared. "Perhaps you could share your building plans with us."

Of course I shared both the vision and infrastructure of the hospital with these distinguished guests and wished them every success as they departed five hours later. Their request was not the first of its kind, nor would it be the last.

It would undoubtedly be possible to replicate the structure of our hospital building in a different location, but Diospi Suyana is so much more than a building, or the expensive equipment it contains. It is the missionary staff, with their sacrificial lifestyle, hard work, and kindness, that makes Diospi Suyana so unique and enticing.

Since we started our work here, we have had more than 180 long-term volunteers. When the hospital first opened, all but one hailed from German-speaking countries. But as I have travelled through Europe and the Americas, our team has become much more diverse. By the spring of 2015, our team represented eleven different nationalities.

Most volunteers come for three years. Some come for five. A few even consider a life-long commitment. They raise their own financial support and forgo their previous, often substantial, salary. These highly motivated men and women are following a call and consider their service in Peru to be an expression of their faith in God. It is one thing to talk about belief, but quite another to do something about it – especially something as drastic as packing up one's entire life and moving overseas.

In this "Me" generation, the term "serve" seems an old-fashioned anomaly. The average person always has an eye out for what's in it for them. People are drawn to safety and comfort, and a bit of luxury. "Giving" usually means a donation at Christmas time and is often done from our excess. It makes us feel good, perhaps a bit righteous. And it costs us very little.

It is quite a different story with our missionaries. They literally risk their lives on a daily basis, sometimes just by coming to work! This is not an exaggeration. Hardly a week goes by without a bus careening off a mountain road and plummeting towards the valley below. In the immediate vicinity of the hospital, there have been four major bus accidents since 2004. Almost every staff member at the hospital can tell you about an accident or near miss they have experienced personally. You may have read in my first book how I narrowly escaped death in a road accident back in 2008. I cannot get life insurance in Germany. Knowing what I do in Peru, insurance companies simply shake their heads. The risk is way too high.

Missionaries march to the beat of a different drum. They willingly make sacrifices every day. They go without the food they are used to. Sometimes they even go without water, such as when the local authorities shut off the neighbourhood supply because of drought! It is no laughing matter to manage without a morning shower.

When life gets hard, there must be faith, a deep conviction, a sense of calling – otherwise there is nothing to prevent them from giving up and going home. Our people are on a "mission" with us, therefore they have earned the classification of "missionaries". Their faith is real, not because of the Scripture they can recite, but because they are willing to put their faith into action. Our patients respect this, many of whom pass other hospitals on their way to us. They don't mind camping out for two or three nights in order to get an appointment. Why? Because they know the reputation of the missionaries, the sacrifices they have made, including getting up in the middle of the night to donate their own blood. They trust their expertise is freely given out of love, not in search of personal gain.

The capitals of many African and South American countries are riddled with well-intentioned international organizations attempting to improve the world through their programmes. I intend no judgment on these programmes or the staff who run them. But please understand that the experience of our missionaries is vastly different. Other aid workers may enjoy air-conditioned offices and a private chauffeur. Their salary may even be higher than it would have been at home, owing to a foreign supplement.

One Sunday, the head of one such German aid organization invited me to his home. It was more of a palace than a house, situated up on a hill, with a beautiful view of the city below. Of course, it was far enough away to avoid the world of the poor. The entire residential area was fenced in, with a guard at the gate to keep away the unwelcome. Our missionaries live by very different standards, on a par with the poor, side by side in their neighbourhoods. People who become missionaries must really be a strange sort, it is often assumed. Perhaps they are just misfits who cannot manage in modern, competitive society. I can assure you this is not the case at Diospi Suyana.

Beginning in 2007, Dr Jens Hassfeld spent five years building up our gynaecology department. Despite all the challenges, his wife Damaris and their four children were fully integrated into Peruvian society.

When the Hassfeld family returned to Germany in 2012 for a year's furlough, Jens was immediately offered a senior consultant position in Bietigheim. How could a doctor climb the ladder of success so quickly? Well, Dr Hassfeld had graduated from medical school with top marks, had an excellent track record in the operating theatre, and was likeable to boot. Regardless, Dr Hassfeld and his family were planning to return to Peru when the year was up.

The local media were on to the potential addition of Dr Hassfeld to the hospital, which essentially had to offer him a permanent contract. With his skills and management qualities, he could have negotiated an even more impressive salary than the one initially offered. He was even offered several extra weeks of annual leave in order to fulfil "his moral obligations in Peru". However tempting any of this might have been, Dr Hassfeld was adamant that he and his family would return to Peru.

On 20 August 2013, I welcomed the Hassfeld family back during our morning worship service. Jens and Damaris have made a deliberate life-long commitment to Diospi Suyana. He has since taken on the role of deputy director of the hospital. At the beginning of 2014, Damaris re-entered the world of paediatric nursing after fifteen years' absence. She is an enormous enrichment to the team and even became head nurse in 2016, a role she plays with a great sense of responsibility.

Missionaries are neither lunatics nor romantics. They give careful consideration to every step and are mindful of the consequences. After all, there is much at stake. As my wife and I were preparing to begin a new life as missionaries in South America, we received commendation but also bitter reproach. We were accused of chasing our own dreams with no thought for our children. All our volunteers have faced similar chastisement.

Daniel Dreßler is a landscape gardener. His wife Susan is an anaesthesiologist. They lived in Curahuasi with their three little boys. Their service at Diospi Suyana was a stark example of just how momentous something as simple as a book dedication can be.

It was Saturday 8 September 2012. I was sharing the story of Diospi Suyana in Rehe, Germany, with representatives of more than 200 bookshops. There was not a single empty chair in the conference room. After my presentation, I situated

122

myself near the door in order to sign copies of my book. I was approached by a certain Frau Herrmann.

"I'll take two books," she said with purpose. "One is for my daughter – she is a doctor."

I enquired about her area of specialization.

"She's an anaesthesiologist in Wismar. Do write a few words of dedication in her book. Her name is Susan Dreßler."

Frau Herrmann was pleased as I complied with her request. It took me no time to come up with the words. We were always short of anaesthesiologists, so I scribed one simple sentence as a cry for help: "Dear Susan, you are needed urgently in Peru!"

Frau Herrmann and her husband read my words prior to giving the book to Susan. Realizing that Susan's reaction might be more than either of them would wish, they made the difficult decision to give her the book on their next visit.

Who doesn't like to get a gift? Susan opened the book flap and read the appeal addressed to her by name. For Susan and her husband, Diospi Suyana became a daily topic of conversation and prayer that autumn.

In the end, Daniel Dreßler decided to visit Diospi Suyana, hoping that first-hand knowledge of the hospital would help them make this life-changing decision. Although flights were exorbitantly expensive at that time, Daniel bought a plane ticket. Two weeks later, Susan received an unexpected bonus at work, which completely covered the cost of the trip.

The Dreßlers wanted to come for at least three and a half years. Their path to Peru, and even in learning the language, has included numerous hurdles. In February 2014, they were interviewed by a reporter from the *Baltic Times* newspaper while studying Spanish in southern Peru. Their responses

GOD HAS SEEN US

to the reporter's questions were painfully honest, including: "When we think of home, the tears start to flow. We miss our family and our friends."

Academics and craftsmen, young and old, optimists and pessimists, Protestants and Catholics, Europeans and Americans – so many have followed God's call to Peru. Some of them had to cope with bad news or injury just as they were leaving home. Tabea Seiler, wife of our former head of administration, was diagnosed with Type II diabetes. Anja Nöh suffered a slipped cervical disc completely unexpectedly. Many would have abandoned their plans for South America, but these families were not deterred. Convinced they had truly been called by God, they got on the plane.

Our new arrivals speak many different languages and have different customs, but despite the cultural, ethnic, and socio-economic differences, they are integrated into the mission community. Journalists often describe Diospi Suyana not as a hospital but as a family, and I think that is fitting. Like all families, we have our occasional differences, but a strong bond connects all our members – not just because we are all pulling in the same direction, but because we all recognize the same One as head of the family. Jesus Christ is Lord in our lives. Theologically speaking, we could say it is not us doing the work, but God working through us. We are His instruments.

This is all a far cry from the increasingly prevalent cultural value of "having it all". But one thing is certain: we may not have bank accounts as thriving as our counterparts in Europe or the USA, but we are happy and our hearts overflow with a sense of purpose.

18

From Kids' Club to Kids' House

Whenever I go for a walk with my wife in Curahuasi, the streets resound with calls of *"Hola, Doctorita!"* (Hello, Doctor Lady!) The warmth in the children's voices and the tenderness in their eyes clearly reveal their deep affection. Most of them know Martina from the Diospi Suyana Kids' Clubs.

Australian Lyndal Maxwell and my wife founded the first Kids' Club in the living room of a private home back in 2005. Games, stories, songs, and sport drew local children like bees to honey. At the club, children not only engaged in fun activities, they also received attention and affirmation.

There are now twelve such clubs running under the Diospi Suyana flag. The weekly sessions are attended by upwards of 400 children. On special occasions such as Christmas, we might see as many as a thousand children. They love the programme, which runs year-round, interrupted only by school holidays.

"Lyndal, what shall I do over the holidays?" lamented one small girl.

She was inconsolable that there would be no club sessions during the school break. The ensuing conversation illuminated why these weekly ninety minutes had become so precious to her.

"I recently prayed there would be no fighting at home," she shared cheerfully. "And for a whole week, there was peace!"

What the kids learn at club they pass on to their parents and siblings. So many families have reported positive changes at home. The truth that God loves all of us just as we are, and is waiting for us to come to Him, is a message shared continuously. It is the best news any of us could ever hear – whether an indigenous child in Curahuasi or a university professor in London. Because if God loves us – me – I am valuable, even if I am growing up in extreme poverty or wasting away in material excess.

When our Kids' House first opened on 16 April 2012, our clubs finally had a proper home for their important work. This was the third Diospi Suyana construction project headed by Udo Klemenz. Both missionaries and locals are heavily involved with this important branch of our work, now under the exemplary leadership of Gladys Illescas.

Indigenous children in the Andes do not lead lives to be envied. At home, they are often witnesses to and victims of physical violence. Many of their parents struggle with alcoholism, putting the children at severe risk of neglect. These are the boys and girls who come to Kids' Club. These are the boys and girls whom Sophia Oester put on stage to perform a musical in Spanish about the life of the apostle Paul. On that glorious day at the end of August 2012, 150 voices of indigenous children filled our amphitheatre with song, the spotlight on them for the first time in their young lives.

The original German lyrics and music were penned by Birgit Minichmayr. She and her husband Hannes founded the KISI Kids' groups in Austria years ago, as a means of carrying the message of faith across borders to young and old alike. These Catholic believers share with Diospi Suyana both faith in God and love for His people.

Who would have thought it, back in 2006 when the amphitheatre was first built, that one day young indigenous children would sing with unbridled joy to the glory of God? And these children, worth nothing at home, were enthusiastically applauded by an audience of 1,500 for their heartfelt performance.

19

New Horizons

School chairs are never the most comfortable, and arriving as a small child from Germany and finding yourself suddenly dropped into a local pre-school in Ecuador comes with a host of additional challenges. Our daughter Natalie was four and her little brother Dominik was two when they were first introduced to a morning pre-school class in Quito. They attended the class as Martina and I began learning Spanish, chewing our way through the bite-sized pieces served up by a private language tutor.

We were initially told by the pre-school staff that our children were very polite – and silent. Not a word passed between their lips. We just hoped that they were absorbing what they were seeing and hearing in their new Spanish-speaking world. And then, after several weeks, their tongues were loosened and they chatted away merrily in Spanish, proving to all that they had successfully made this transition to South America.

When we started working as mission doctors there in 1999, we sent Natalie and Dominik to the local school. They wore the same uniforms, sat at the same decrepit tables, and complained about the same homework as their Ecuadorian peers.

Autumn 2003 marked a new era as we crossed over into neighbouring Peru to build Diospi Suyana in the Apurímac region. Our children, of which there were now three, were soon right at home in the Peruvian culture. They sang the national anthem at school with such fervour you might have thought the country needed liberating from Spain all over again. Like their peers, they developed a certain contempt for Chile, which had annexed a part of southern Peru during the War of the Pacific (1879–84). At public fiestas, they joined in the folk dancing, wearing bright traditional dress just like their classmates. Hopping and jumping across the square like little Incas, they kept perfect time to the songs, a feat often difficult for Europeans owing to the more complicated rhythms.

If there had been any caution or reserve between us parents and the local population, our children crashed right through it. The indigenous women would call out to Tina at the market, "*Doctorita*, we never could have imagined that your children would dance like ours!"

Natalie, Dominik, and Florian may have had a German surname, but to all intents and purposes they were becoming Peruvian – a development Tina and I were most delighted about.

We paid no mind to the sad state of the local school building, nor to the unusual teaching methods. Of course, we – particularly Tina – noted that rote learning and copying textbook pages played a significant role in the learning process here, whereas creativity and logic were not particularly encouraged. Appearances, however, were important. Our children stood in the schoolyard each morning, uniform immaculate, and marched in perfect step with their class: chest out, stomach in, legs straight and lifted high as they stared straight ahead – our three offspring marching in the middle of the ranks like Peruvian patriots.

GOD HAS SEEN US

Teachers were not what you might call "punctual", and discipline did not appear to be high on their list of priorities. When the classroom got out of hand, they often reached for the cane to re-establish some semblance of order and their authority.

One lunchtime, as we ate soup in our kitchen, Natalie blurted out, "Today the teacher rapped us all on the fingers, but it didn't hurt!"

Astounded, I nearly dropped my spoon. A raging teacher punishing the whole class and hitting my precious daughter was enough to ruin my appetite.

"What is this man's name?" I demanded, staring Natalie in the eye.

"Papa, please don't make a fuss. I'm not telling you his name."

I jumped up from the table and rushed to the car, despite the protest of my children. They were mortified by the serious chiding I was about to give the school principal. When I returned to the table some time later, they wasted no time schooling me in the error of my ways.

"Papa, you're impossible! What will the other kids say now?"

The teaching methods at the school in Curahuasi left much to be desired, but of far more concern was the entire country's poor performance in the Programme for International Student Assessment (PISA). In 2012, Peru managed to come last in all three performance measures – a fact that somehow did not seem to trouble the Ministry of Education for very long.

Despite the cane, the miserably low standards, and the below-par facilities, Tina and I were depending on this opportunity for our children to become integrated in our Peruvian community. In that respect, things really could not have gone any better. Natalie, Dominik, and Florian were all regularly invited to birthday parties, and none of the other children appeared bothered by the slightly lighter skin tone of the *gringitos*, as our children were affectionately called.

In the evenings, my wife helped our children with German correspondence courses. In my honest opinion, these lessons were incredibly challenging. The thick textbooks were daunting in themselves. But fortunately I had had the good sense to marry Tina, and she had this home-schooling thing worked out. How she had the energy to guide our children through such rigorous academia after a gruelling day at the hospital is beyond me. But somehow she managed to motivate Natalie, Dominik, and Florian to learn. Our children were ultimately successful in every single school they attended – whether in Germany, Ecuador, Peru, or the USA. I credit two factors: the intelligence given to them by God and the dedicated support they received at home from their mother.

The other missionary families who had joined us at Diospi Suyana also had their doubts about the local schools. Most of them intended to stay just a short period of time but were nevertheless gravely concerned that their children would not progress academically, and would bear the consequences of their Andes village school experience for the rest of their school career. Was the mission experience an adventure or an ego trip for the parents, at the unacceptable price of their children's education? The call for a decent school for the missionary children grew louder and louder.

Tina and I maintained our position, encouraging families to send their children to the local school as we did.

But they began to distance themselves from us, literally as well as figuratively. They returned to Europe as soon as their three-year commitment was fulfilled.

"We would have liked to stay longer," they said. "But our children don't like their school and neither do we!"

Something had to be done. People were voting with their feet, and we needed to take some serious action if we wanted to retain missionaries at Diospi Suyana. As I travel for half the year sharing the story of Diospi Suyana, I am always hopeful of recruiting new staff, but it is inarguably much easier to keep the staff you have than to attract new ones from so far away. Tina and I were not going to be able to escape the idea of a missionary school.

Two and a half months after we opened the dental clinic, Tina and I finally managed a mini-break to Urubamba, in the sacred valley of the Incas. Our grand plan entailed simply catching up on sleep. Our children would manage on their own for the weekend, with light telephone "encouragement" to remain sensible during this period of freedom.

On the Saturday morning, 11 September 2010, my wife and I were merrily trekking along one of the local trails, the breath-taking mountain scenery and bright blue sky rejuvenating our spirits.

"Let's hike up to the snowline," I joked, regarding the 15,000-feet peak above us.

Of course, we hadn't made the trip to engage in "extreme sports". Our goal was to have some uninterrupted time to think and dialogue together – and that is what we did. Passionately. The next two hours unfurled into a brainstorming session of the finest quality. We shared our dreams for the hospital, our

GOD HAS SEEN US

children, and the rest of our lives. And we debated the pros and cons of a Diospi Suyana school.

By the time we had wiped our feet at the door of our guest house, the decision was firmly made. Tina and I would do everything we could to establish a modern school in Curahuasi, and it would be open to local and missionary children alike. We would use education as a tool to improve society – that was our declared intention. As believers in Christ, the teachers would be not only first-class educators, but also inspiring role models, living out an authentic faith. And missionaries would at last have a quality school to which they could send their children, thus increasing the attraction of Diospi Suyana for young families.

Tina lay in bed flipping through a novel, while I sat at the simple wooden table drafting the first two pages of our project outline. Eight and a half years earlier, we had put pen to paper on the plans for the Diospi Suyana hospital. Now it was time for a school. As before, we were completely reliant on God. He was the originator, the architect, the builder, the boss. As it says in the Bible, we are to commit all we do unto the Lord (Proverbs 16:3).

I pressed the "save" button on my laptop and read my clever proposition to Tina. No doubt about it, the school had just come into being. We could already see it in our mind's eye. We smiled, sensing the familiar throbbing of our hearts that registered the start of something truly extraordinary. It was time for a school – the when, where, and how were just minor details that God would make clear in His own good time.

It would be another year before I got to page 3 of the written project plan, but even during this writing hiatus, we kept moving forward towards the goal. In July 2011, Diospi

GOD HAS SEEN US

Suyana in Germany voted during its annual general meeting to extend the scope of the mission and ratified this decision through constitutional amendment.

In September we acquired an 8,500 m^2 plot of land in Curahuasi. It was pleasantly green, flat, and available for a reasonable local rate. After negotiations were complete, we transferred $220,000 to the owners. Now we had the land; we just needed the building.

At this point in time, Udo Klemenz was fully engaged in building our third project, the Diospi Suyana Kids' House. However, one evening I spotted him eyeing the land we had just acquired. I knew that glint in his eye – I had seen it many times before. If our engineer was already showing interest in this old anise field, I knew he would be more than willing to head up construction of the school with his usual professionalism, passion, and dedication.

20

The Willing

Not every mountain is ours to climb, nor is every good work part of our calling. Discernment is critical as we consider which responsibilities to take on while we have the strength to do so. But who makes the final choice? Is it just us, or do others play a part?

When we recite the Lord's Prayer on Sunday mornings and get to the line "Thy will be done", perhaps not all of us give thought to what that might really mean – what *is* God's will for our lives? Most people agree that we should behave ourselves – don't cheat, do good, shun evil, and try to be a good person. My wife and I are certain that the will of God is not limited to these general ideas, but is revealed to be radically personal. What does God want of us? He must have had some idea when He made us with our unique gifts as well as challenges.

The acceptance of this concept really does depend on our personal degree of faith in a God who knows and loves us. Many people are positively bewildered by the thought. They think God sets things in motion, then indifferently sits back to watch – if He even exists at all.

Tina and I were absolutely clear that not only was the school a good idea, but it was our job to make it happen. But how did we know? To be sure, there were numerous practical reasons for such a massive project, but the deep peace we experienced within as we stepped forward was much more indicative of the proper path being taken. If our feelings were correct, we knew God would place His blessing on the work. But faith must be more than feelings, or "warm-fuzzies". The true test is where the rubber meets the road, so to speak. I will leave you to decide whether God provided His holy support in building our school.

I value the wisdom of others. I often wonder if God is speaking to me through them. In the course of the last twenty years, I have been guided in this manner many times.

At the urging of John and Viola Lentink, Diospi Suyana hospital staff, on 1 November 2011 I drove from Wiesbaden to Lauf an der Pegnitz to visit Cornelius and Tina Linder. The Linders ran their own architecture firm and were most open to hearing the Diospi Suyana story.

During my one-hour presentation, Tina positively beamed and her husband kept nodding in affirmation. Given their capability and obvious enthusiasm for our work, the Linders could be a powerful force to have on board.

I cleared my throat and braved the question: "Would you be willing to draw up the building plans – at no charge?"

"That would be possible," Frau Linder answered thoughtfully.

Her husband added, "We have already designed a school for poor children in Ethiopia, and we even headed up the construction team on site."

They were both well aware of the extensive time and effort required to draft such building plans. We wanted a quality school that could serve up to 600 children. The value of such a property could easily approach $3 million. And yet the Linders appeared extremely motivated to support the cause of Diospi Suyana. No doubt they had checked out the website before our meeting that day.

"Yes, you can count us in!" they declared.

I took their response as a definite promise and immediately suggested we be on a first-name basis with one another.

As Tina Linder was to confess to me later, at times the planning was so complicated and extensive, she and her husband essentially spent half of their working hours on the Diospi Suyana school plans. They were a small company, just a husband and wife team. Financially speaking, donating so much time to us cost them dearly. Yet they were resolute in keeping their word. By the time the last line was drawn and the last measurements calculated, they had donated approximately €100,000 worth of work.

Structural engineer Jürgen Engel from Mettingen provided additional technical and planning support. He never sent a bill, saving us another €35,000. He had read my first book, *I Have Seen God*, and understood that the work of Diospi Suyana was not something on which a price could easily be fixed. His generous donation of hours and expertise is yet another example of how hearts have been moved by the spreading of this powerful story of faith.

During the first week of June 2012, Udo and Barbara Klemenz unpacked their bags in Curahuasi for the fourth time. After successful completion of the hospital, dental clinic, and Kids' House, Udo would now be overseeing construction of the school. We had not negotiated a salary. He again would be sacrificially giving his extraordinary skill completely free of charge, thus saving Diospi Suyana another €100,000. Neither he nor I would ever discuss this remarkable gesture of generosity.

On 15 June 2012, Udo Klemenz submitted his first building report, detailing the progress made on the school. I posted it on our website with the apt headline "Tried and Tested Voice Reports Back In". A hundred more reports followed, one per week, as the construction crew raised a racket in the otherwise peaceful valley of Curahuasi. The diggers rolled in, the trucks delivered cement and sand, and the heavy machinery roared through their heavy work. The dry season had begun and the sun shone brightly in the sky. Everything seemed to be going just perfectly.

During the last week of June, I began to hear rumblings that the local government would be requiring us to pay for a building permit. I was immediately alarmed. If that decision was made, there would be no way to appeal. A permit could cost us up to 1.5 per cent of the total construction costs – an amount I estimated to be close to $50,000. Normally, it would take more than fifty presentations in clubs and churches to raise that kind of money. There really was no justification for the town hall to seek this payment, as our project was of a charitable nature. However, I was going to need to clarify this for our presiding mayor.

On 4 July 2012, I sat in a guest house in Lima, tracking our daughter Natalie's flight online so I could pick her up from the airport upon arrival. Our seventeen-year-old daughter was attending high school in Wiesbaden and was coming to visit us during her summer break. With concern, I noted that her flight from Frankfurt had been delayed, therefore she would probably miss her connection in Madrid.

Later that evening, I was able to Skype with Natalie as she waited in Madrid. She told me that LAN Airlines had given her seat to another passenger, even though the flight from Frankfurt had actually arrived on time. She was now in a hotel and unclear as to how she would be able to proceed to Lima.

I was so frustrated. I had been missing Natalie for months now, and had been so looking forward to gathering her in my arms upon her arrival. I am one of those parents who tend to worry about their children, and now it seemed justified. Neither Natalie nor LAN could tell me when she would be arriving in Lima. How annoying! Hopefully no harm would befall my daughter, who was still a minor, while she waited in Madrid. I prayerfully committed her to God's loving care. As there was clearly no point in going to the airport now, I considered what else I might do while in Lima.

On the off-chance he might be available, I gave the mayor of Curahuasi a call on my mobile. I had heard a rumour that he might be in Lima for business. The rumour was apparently accurate, and Señor Vergara Abarca answered the phone immediately.

"Señor Mayor," I began, "I happen to be in the capital too. May I please speak with you this evening at your hotel? I'd like to show you some photos."

Shakespeare's Julius Caesar claimed he preferred the company of obese people, as they seemed more content and therefore pleasant to have around. If one ascribed to this view, one might conclude that Señor Abarca was an extremely pleasant person – and they would not be wrong.

"Of course, Dr John! Please come at 7:30."

As my taxi pulled up outside his hotel, I recognized with respect and gratitude as a taxpayer that the mayor was staying at a modestly priced hotel. We sat down together at a table. His legal advisor joined us. I had said I wanted to show the mayor a few photos. This was a blatant understatement, as I actually intended to take him through the entire hour-long tale of Diospi Suyana.

As I concluded, I thanked the mayor for bearing with me and awaited his response.

"Dr John, I am grateful for all you and your people have done for our district. You have my complete support!"

This was exactly the reply I had been hoping for. "Señor Mayor, I do in fact need your assistance. As you know, we are building a school, and we do not have the money in hand to pay for a building permit. Will you please give us exemption from this charge?"

The mayor nodded emphatically, and repeatedly stated that he would do so. Had the mayor just become trapped by his own words, or had the story of Diospi Suyana truly touched his heart? I did not know for sure and I didn't want to leave the matter unsettled.

"Then, Señor Mayor, let's seal this deal with a handshake and I will post the photo on our website!"

The mayor's legal advisor also proved adept at photography. Before midnight, picture evidence of our agreement was uploaded to the internet.

Señor Abarca kept his word. At his direction, the local council let us off the full $50,000 building permit amount, without questions or conditions. Looking back, I am grateful to God that Natalie missed her connection in Spain that night. An inconvenience opened the door to blessing. You will surely agree with me that the encounter with the mayor was nothing short of miraculous. And that word accurately describes pretty much the entire progression of our school project.

On 20 March 2013, I reported to reception at Nora Flooring Solutions in Weinheim. Nora's rubber flooring is likely the best available on the world market. Four members of staff from the Export and Public Relations departments were waiting for me. They took me to a small display area and showed me a flooring sample that had given thirty years of faithful service at Frankfurt airport and still looked like new.

I started at the very beginning of the Diospi Suyana story and concluded with a petition for our current need of floor covering. The people from Nora, and their head of sales, Gilbert Gourdin, in particular, knew immediately that the Diospi Suyana school needed a high-performance Nora floor. I agreed completely – also aware that the cost of the 2,000 m^2 we needed would be nearly $80,000.

After the meeting, Herr Gourdin walked me out to my rental car. On the way, we talked not of prices, gift aid receipts, or export challenges, but about the unseen world that meant more to us than corporate success or huge bank accounts ever could.

A few weeks later, Gilbert Gourdin gave me a dismaying update: the company management had not approved the donation of floor covering for our school. The directors had frowned, not understanding what Nora Europe had to do with a school in the Andes. The simple answer was that it had nothing to do with it. And that was that. Dismissed.

Such decisions by executives focused on profit are no surprise. It's the way the world works. Idealism and dreaming cost money, and there is just no room for that kind of thinking in the budget. It's not logical. But Gilbert Gourdin understood that much happens between heaven and earth that confounds human logic.

The rubber flooring arrived in Peru, delivered without an invoice, PR attention, or really any fuss at all. Herr Gourdin had somehow managed to convince the Nora executives that it would be in the company's best interests to consider our school a "test site" and proceed with shipping the flooring. How he managed that is a mystery he took to his grave; he died quite suddenly of acute hepatitis C in September 2014.

Change of scene. The date is 13 May 2012. I had just finished a presentation at a church in Bad Zwischenahn. A woman in the front row gave an audible sigh of appreciation. It was a warm spring day, and most of my audience did not waste time in making their exit into the sunshine. I was just packing up when suddenly Pastor Lothar Bublitz from Bremen appeared in front of me.

"What are you doing here?" I asked in amazement. "I haven't seen you for years!"

"I am here with my daughter Michaela," he answered. "She would like to do some work experience with you in Peru."

Diospi Suyana is flooded with similar requests and we usually have to respond with a letter of gentle rejection. But Lothar and his daughter had travelled a full hour across northern Germany to make their request in person. Lothar had also helped us back in 2004 by facilitating the transfer of a rather large inheritance. I knew I was going to have to make an exception, especially as his daughter was a highly qualified young woman.

"I'll see what I can do," I responded sincerely, shaking both their hands.

"Oh, and there is something else," Lothar continued. "You really should look into BILD helps – A Heart for Children. They gave us a grant to build our kindergarten."

I have a pretty active imagination, as anyone who knows me will attest to. Still, asking the *BILD* newspaper for support was something I could not wrap my brain around.

The *BILD* newspaper is the most widely read tabloid in Europe. I'm not sure if the appeal comes from its gossip, coarse language, and sensationalism, or the abundance of underdressed women depicted in photos throughout each edition. Regardless, a partnership between *BILD* and Diospi Suyana seemed rather incongruous.

Two weeks later, I was in Udo Klemenz's office, sharing this absurd idea. We couldn't help but grin at the paradox, but at the same time I recalled an old saying about leaving no stone unturned. I sensed a gentle urging, a realization that just maybe God had sent Lothar Bublitz to Bad Zwischenahn with this suggestion.

When Pastor Bublitz forwarded me the application forms a few days later, I got straight to work filling in the required details. Udo and I drew up a financial plan, as it makes no sense to ask for support when you don't know how much you will need. And there we were – in the middle of building and yet without a detailed financial plan. As I attempted to describe our plan, I made it clear that my wife and I were not relying on our own limited resources, but opening our hands to the power and generosity of the Almighty God. On page 9 I closed with the following sentence: "We would like to apply for a grant in the amount of €240,000, which is approximately 10 per cent of our projected costs. We are certain that the Colegio Diospi Suyana will be built through God's help, and we would like to invite BILD helps to be part of this dream."

BILD helps responded to our invitation with the utmost enthusiasm. Frau Krüger, head of the foundation, was so touched by Diospi Suyana that she rallied the rest of her team to support us. They voted unanimously to award a grant for the amount we had requested. The money was transferred in three instalments and was immediately transformed into cement, steel, and roofing materials. After such generous support, I thought perhaps I should subscribe to the *BILD* as a small gesture of gratitude. I will continue to think about this for the rest of my life.

If you are a Christian, the next account might surprise you. It was Monday 13 May 2013. I was driving across southern Germany to speak with a group of students in Ulm. Following up on a recommendation, I placed a call to the WPU Company in Illtertissen and requested an appointment while I was in the area. WPU constructs high-quality workshops for schools, and I hoped we might obtain their support in supplying our school with such a workshop. The sales representative on the phone had no problem with me coming to the office to meet him. I had judiciously not mentioned that I was hoping to discuss a possible donation.

After a quick stop for breakfast, I arrived slightly late at WPU, where I learned that the sales representative had already left for his next appointment. I felt a bit stood up, but in the absence of the sales representative, the owner Michael Kiehl attended to me himself. It almost seemed as though he had been expecting me, as he allowed me to set up the laptop for my presentation.

"What you have there in Peru is fantastic," he praised, as I was setting up. "But as far as your faith is concerned, I'm afraid I am going to disappoint you. I am a practising Buddhist and recently met with the Dalai Lama!"

Above: The Diospi Suyana hospital in the high-lying valley of Curahuasi – for many a little piece of heaven on earth.

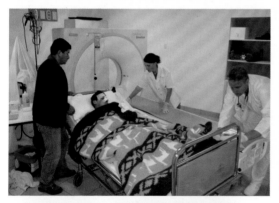

Left: Must be a record! On 25 January 2010 our hard-working staff carried out 148 X-rays and CT scans. L to R: Computer expert Benjamin Azuero, radiographer Esther Lietzau and paediatrician Dr Armin Frick.

26 January 2010: Transferring the first two patients by helicopter. L to R: Dr Oliver Engelhard, Dr David Brady, nurse Michael Mörl and intensive care nurses Karin Wettstein and Stefan Höfer.

Above: Falling down the mountainside, Karin Wettstein landed on this roof – the only building within two and a half miles.

Below: Dentist Dr Dankfried Geister and his wife high above the Atlantic on 24 August 2008, after sharing the Diospi Suyana film on their laptop.

Above: Alexandra Kopp, Marit Weilbach, and Stefan Höfer taking part in the folklore dance.

Inauguration ceremony of the dental clinic on 26 June 2010. The evildoers Karius and Baktus are knocking holes into teeth.

Pilar Nores (blonde lady on the right), Jörg Vogel from Sirona and Ayla Bloomberg from Henry Schein stand behind the model of the clinic.

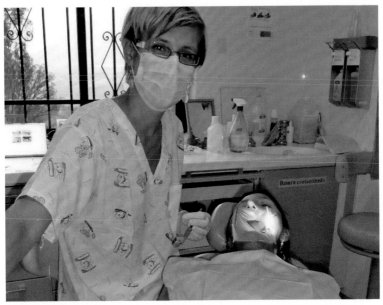

Dentist Dr Marlen Luckow at work in the dental clinic.

First operation by eye specialist Dr Ursula Buck at the Diospi Suyana hospital. The patient is a Quechua man, who was hospitalized after a bull rammed its horn into his eye.

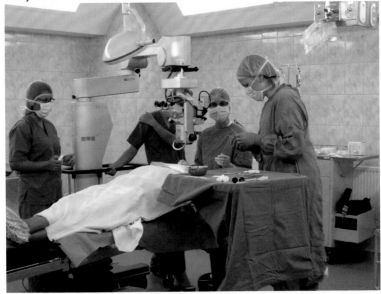

Top: 21 April 2010: Presentation in front of top politicians from all of the parties represented in the Peruvian congress. Shaking hands with Dr Alva Castro, president of the Chamber of Deputies.

Left: At the Ziehl-Abegg stand at the Augsburg elevator fair on 11 October 2009.

Bottom: The first official ride in the donated elevator. On the left is Wolf-Dietrich Schreier, on the right in the blue shirt Michael Mörl.

Right: Dental technician Lisa Isaak in the lab. Lisa served for three years at the clinic.

Above: 10 March 2013. On the final evening of ProChrist I was interviewed by Jürgen Werth, a well-known Christian broadcaster and songwriter. More than 100,000 viewers in 800 locations were watching via satellite.

Left: Olaf Böttger and Volker Kauder from the German government on the day of the cheque presentation.

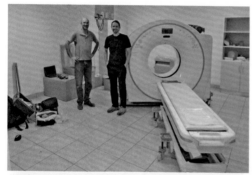

26 June 2014: Markus Rolli and Wolfgang Wenisch installing the new Hitachi CT scanner.

The authorities had the contents of container 32 taken out and put back in five times.

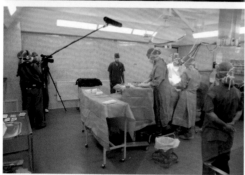

A Deutsche Welle camera team preparing a television documentary that was broadcast worldwide in November 2013 in English, Spanish, German and Arabic.

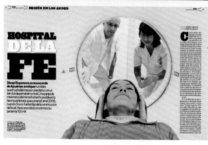

The first double-page spread in the *SOMOS* report on 16 February 2013 showing our 100,000th patient in the CT scanner.

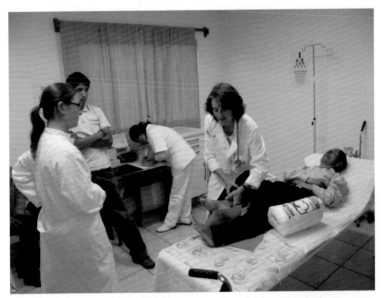

My wife examining a patient's leg as a German medical student looks on.

When I am not on the road or at my desk I carry out gastroscopies and colonoscopies. Here I am training English medical student Ruth Brand.

Hospital head of administration Stefan Seiler, with his wife Tabea and their children Olivia and Robin, who left for Peru despite the fact that Tabea had been diagnosed with Type II diabetes shortly beforehand.

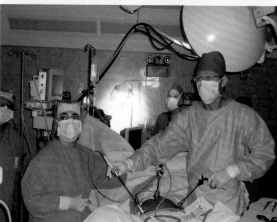

Gynaecologist Dr Jens Hassfeld performing laparoscopic surgery.

Below: 28 July 2014: Several members of staff who participated in the public parade in Curahuasi on Peru's national holiday.

Right: Udo Klemenz and his wife Barbara lived in Peru for nine years. He headed up almost all of our construction projects until 2019.

Below: 16 April 2012: The Diospi Suyana Kids' House is inaugurated.

31 August 2012: Sophia Oester puts on a children's musical on the big stage in the amphitheatre. The children and their parents loved it.

Above: 26 January 2012: Architects Cornelius and Tina Linder share their plans for the Diospi Suyana school.

Above: The Bigalke family in Arrivals at Lima airport on 16 September 2013.

Right: Social worker Carolin Klett (photo) and teacher Julianna Rolli visited more than 200 families.

On 14 March 2014, 800 guests celebrated the inauguration of the Diospi Suyana school.

Teaching staff on the Colégio's big day.

Pupils at the Diospi Suyana school express their thanks to Udo Klemenz.

The Diospi Suyana school, with the outline of the hospital in the background.

Left: Christine Fleck from Kirchheimbolanden raised more than €60,000 by selling granola made in her own kitchen.

Graphic designer Bernd Schermuly from Wiesbaden invested more than 100 hours' worth of work in the new Diospi Suyana website. And never sent us a bill.

President Ollanta Humala (in the red poncho) shortly after landing on the hospital helipad.

5 June 2014: An audience with the Peruvian president Ollanta Humala and his wife Nadine Heredia. On the left, Dr Jens Hassfeld; on the right, my wife and me.

My first book in the window of the Leben und Lesen bookshop in Wiesbaden.

Right: Janet Yachoua translated my book into English free of charge.

Below: 6 May 2014: Visiting Professor John Lennox in his office in Oxford.

During my presentation to the Young Nursing Professionals on 7 May 2013.

On 13 October 2013, I gave the Special Lecture at the 4th World Congress of Pediatric Surgery in Berlin.

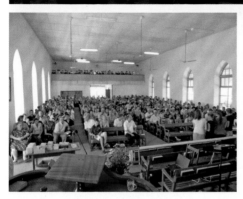

White African Adrian Gibson prepared my UK tour in exemplary fashion.

17 February 2013: Shortly before my presentation at a church in the Chaco of Paraguay. The room was packed and more people were following the talk outside.

Below: The chest of drawers is a perfect fit.

Above: Sometimes there are so many patients wanting an appointment that they camp out at the main entrance.

Right: The mission hospital waiting room is packed full (126 seats).

Right: The John family in July 2014. Standing at the back: Dominik, Natalie, and Florian; seated in front: my wife and me.

Hello, I thought. *That's interesting.* Now we would see how he responded to my own profession of faith, which is a part of every presentation.

"Yes, we will donate a workshop to your school. We can manage that!" he offered in an assuring, resonant tone. "We might even be able to inspire other companies to help you."

I expressed my sincere gratitude and we agreed to keep in touch.

Several months passed and I was beginning to wonder whether Michael Kiehl would keep his word. Then I received a very promising email from Herr Kiehl, which included a detailed list of fittings and tools that his company would be donating to our school. I was absolutely flabbergasted and soaked up the details of the list several times, as one might do a long-awaited love letter.

Michael Kiehl told the owner of Schneider's Joinery in Waldstetten about the WPU donation to Diospi Suyana. Christoph Schneider was equally inspired and sent twenty-seven new office cupboards for the school. What was donated either by Herr Kiehl directly or as a result of his influence exceeded a value of €20,000.

Over the years, the most unexpected people have joined our growing list of supporters. My jaw has hit the floor many times over the way God has used all types – Christians and atheists, Buddhists and Jews, agnostics and New-Agers, optimists and pessimists, altruists and egotists, the enthusiastic and the reticent – all to advance His glorious kingdom through the work of Diospi Suyana.

When I speak to people about Diospi Suyana, I always make it abundantly clear that I am a follower of Christ. I will not hide this fact just to win the support of someone with a

GOD HAS SEEN US

different belief system. I continue to hope that each person who hears the Diospi Suyana story will recognize the hand of God throughout.

Ten years ago, I heard an inspiring assertion during a Christian management conference: "A vision is good if it totally fulfils us, serves many people, and honours God." I try to keep that in mind every step of the way. My wife and I are utterly passionate about Diospi Suyana, and we want to light that fire in others as well.

Nobody would dispute the fact that the Diospi Suyana hospital – and now the school – is a great blessing to the region. In everything we say and do, it is our deepest desire to point people towards our living God. Our audiences seem to sense this, and deep in their hearts something begins to stir. Maybe they can't quite name it, but that is what makes what unfolds all the more amazing.

21

Wanted: Headteacher

I am glad my own school days were finished more than forty years ago. But since I often share my presentations in schools, I have the opportunity to observe the pandemonium up close, at no risk to my person, of course – a bit like a trip to the zoo. With no need to fear an impending maths test, I saunter down the long corridors that in my youth would have no doubt intimidated me. Should the headmaster appear suddenly, I can politely greet him without shaking in my shoes.

Truthfully, I feel more empathy for headteachers than I do for pupils these days. They bear the brunt of responsibility for nearly everything that goes awry, even though it is rarely directly their fault. When all the students and teachers have gone home, the headteacher remains, all alone in the office, writing difficult letters, modifying the curriculum, responding politely to challenging parents, and respectfully tolerating criticism from the local education authority. If someone is looking for an easy life, they should definitely avoid becoming a headteacher. Perhaps the greatest pressure on a headteacher comes from within, as they know the reputation of their school is very much a reflection of their own leadership abilities.

For this reason, we were looking for a first-rate headteacher for the Diospi Suyana school – perhaps the best one ever. We were offering our usual attractive salary and benefits package, meaning the position would need to be filled on a completely voluntary basis. A few people expressed lukewarm interest in the job, but to be honest I was unsure any of them had the dedication and resilience to commit to a foreign school in the Peruvian mountains.

On 19 September 2012, I gave a presentation at a Protestant church in Bornheim. Nurse Tabea Fröhlich was preparing to join us in Peru and had invited me to speak at her church prior to her departure. Towards the end of the presentation, I included a few photos of the Diospi Suyana school under construction. The idea of possibility hit Christian Bigalke like a bolt of lightning.

Christian Bigalke was a high-school Spanish teacher from Wüfrath with no particular connection to this church or town. He had found himself in the middle of my audience that day because he had a friend who had recently moved to Bornheim, and Christian had come to visit in the hope of helping his friend find a new church home.

He was hooked as soon as the first photos lit up the screen. His thoughts went to a study trip he had taken to Nicaragua back in 2002. There he had met Pastor Oscar Cortez. One afternoon, Pastor Cortez invited him to go for a ride.

"Christian, there is something I must show you!"

This was the only explanation offered for the trip. After a short drive along winding and dirty roads, they pulled up in front of a dilapidated building on the edge of town. Both men climbed out of the car.

"You know, Christian, with God's help it is my dream to turn this old factory into a school for poor children!" the young pastor declared, eyes glistening with emotion as

148

he regarded the old building that anyone else would have condemned.

Christian looked from the deteriorating walls and broken window panes to the glowing face of the man who had brought him there. Immediately, it was as though scales had fallen from his eyes and he could see the real purpose behind his being there. Heading up a school for disadvantaged children was not just the hope of a local pastor. In that very moment it became Christian's life purpose as well. As for where and when, time would tell.

Christian Bigalke approached me at the end of my presentation. The few brief words he shared about his life caught my attention. I felt strongly that his calling to head up a school for poor children was real. His determination was palpable, and I began to sense I was in the presence of the future headteacher of the Diospi Suyana school.

For ten years Christian had held this aspiration, not knowing when it would come to fruition. His wife Verena had held the same hope in her heart for eighteen years. She had been in Rwanda in 1994 on a humanitarian mission, and had witnessed first-hand indescribable human cruelty. A million people, Hutus and Tutsi, were now dead. Murdered in a rampage of terror and bloodlust. As a Christian teacher, surrounded by newly orphaned children with sad eyes mirroring their inner desperation, Verena began to suspect what God had in mind for her future.

There are a number of places in the Bible where the authors use the expression "When the time had fully come…". For example, long before the birth of Jesus, the prophet Isaiah foreshadowed the Lamb who would be slain in heart-rending detail. Some 800 years later, the prophecy came to pass and

Christ was crucified, as "the time had fully come". Everything is in God's time. He may plant a seed or give a signal, and then we wait – until all of a sudden things start to happen very quickly. So it was for the Bigalkes.

Two days later, we met again in Halle. This time, Christian had brought his wife along so that she too could hear the story of Diospi Suyana for herself. Before I even began the presentation, they handed me their application documents and impressive CVs enclosed in fine folders, one red, one blue, so that I did not mix them up. I am always grateful for any such assistance, no matter how small!

Christiane Gerner, from the local Halle newspaper, came along half an hour before the scheduled presentation. She asked me a few questions about Diospi Suyana, then snapped some photos. Under the headline "We Trust in God", an article appeared in the 26 September edition of the paper, accompanied by a large picture of two ecstatic Bigalkes and one very grateful mission doctor. This essentially cemented position offers for both the Bigalkes before they had even been interviewed. Thousands of readers learned from their daily paper that for these two educators "the time had fully come".

Practically every German teacher dreams of achieving *Beamten* status. This is a special qualification for which they must apply, and they are reclassified as an employee of the German government rather than of the school. *Beamte*, or civil servant, status comes with all kinds of benefits, such as an increased pension and access to private health insurance. But the biggest perk is the job security. Assuming a teacher does nothing blatantly illegal, their job is safe for life – an important consideration, especially during an economic

150

GOD HAS SEEN US

crisis. Christian Bigalke was one of those lucky *Beamte* German teachers.

Such civil servants must, of course, fulfil their responsibilities. They cannot just take off on a whim and expect to return to their position later. *Beamte* status is not for quitters. The government gets seriously annoyed when a deserter is discovered in its otherwise obedient ranks.

When Christian told his supervisor at the Carl Fuhlrott School about his plans to go to Peru, he looked at him as though he had lost his mind.

"Herr Bigalke, that is career suicide!" the headteacher warned from behind his desk. His perturbed expression was a clear caution against throwing away hard-won status for a castle in the air.

Christian nodded imperceptibly. He knew his boss was right. Disappearing to South America for a few years would destroy his respected professional status. But sometimes Christians come to these crossroads. When it is clear what God wants them to do, they choose His path, no matter what the risk. A successful career, job security, a healthy bank balance – who doesn't want these things? But for a Christian, they are not the ultimate goal. Christian knew what he had to do, and was willing to do it.

To be quite honest, these are the people I am most happy to have on staff at Diospi Suyana. Mission means dedication and sacrifice. Mission isn't just an opportunity to cool one's heels until an academic placement is offered. Mission isn't an escape from a stressful home or something to fill the time during a period of unemployment. Mission costs. Becoming a missionary involves welcoming hardship and challenge, eschewing comfort and security, putting absolute faith in the

151

One who called out 2,000 years ago, "If anyone would come after me, let him deny himself and take up his cross and follow me." (Matthew 16:24, *ESV*)

Still, Christian Bigalke felt it was wise to ask questions and see what his options for retaining his professional status might be. He made an appointment at the regional government offices and submitted an official request for unpaid leave.

"How long are you planning to be in Peru?" the ladies and gentlemen of the reviewing panel enquired, a note of pity in their smiles.

"At least five years," Christian answered softly.

"That's impossible!" Their negative response reverberated through the hall. "There is no legal basis for retaining your status after such a long time."

Now I really must congratulate Christian Bigalke on several of his personal characteristics. The man has patience and endurance, and he is most persistent. For five long months, he appealed to the school authorities with such courtesy and respect that they could not have acted against him without risking consequences themselves. Concurrently, Christian and Verena were asking God for a solution. They knew that He could say yes, even when the local authorities were shouting no.

What eventually transpired was truly unique. After six months of petitioning, a clerk discovered a bit of a loophole. She found a paragraph in the North Rhine Westphalia regulations that stated a teacher could be permitted to take up to twelve years' unpaid leave in order to raise his or her children.

Fortunately, Christian and Verena are the parents of two lovely little girls, Maryse and Lisanne. The girls were over the

GOD HAS SEEN US

moon that Daddy had taken twelve years off work just to raise them. He would also be serving as the headteacher at a school in Peru...but that was just a happy coincidence.

22

Down to the Wire

Week by week, Udo Klemenz faithfully submitted his building progress reports, which I uploaded to our website each Friday. His reports were written in such clear detail that any reasonably competent DIY enthusiast could have replicated our school in his own country.

To keep our costs down, I sought donated materials both in Peru and abroad. PERI GmbH of Weißenhorn, provided formwork and lent us scaffolding systems for the duration of the construction phase. The use of such materials would normally cost $100,000, but PERI charged us nothing.

CELIMA, a Peruvian company, donated ceramic tiles for the walls and floors. All of our lighting, worth $25,000, was provided by JOSFEL in Lima. The owner of JOSFEL, Jorge Luis Feliu, had previously given us all the lighting for our hospital in 2007. All he asked for in return was a tax receipt!

Just before Christmas in 2013, I travelled to Lima to present our work to a group of Catholic businessmen. Given the usual Christmas hustle and bustle, only twelve men managed to appear at the Maria Reina church that day. We all joined hands as we recited the Lord's Prayer at the end of our time together. The men commended our work, and wished me great success and God's blessing.

One man, Hektor Dasso, was more of a quiet type. Without any fuss, he simply handed me his business card and promised to cover the transportation costs for one container of school furniture and building materials. I had just told the men that there were three containers to transport from Lima to Curahuasi, each at a rate of roughly $5,000.

Throughout my lifetime, I have been on the receiving end of numerous empty promises. After two weeks, I began to fear that Hektor Dasso's statement was just one more. But I was wrong. On 6 January I received an email from him.

"Dear Klaus," Señor Dasso began, "I have just been on holiday with my family. I took your book about Diospi Suyana with me. Once I started to read, I could not put it down. I have no words to describe this work. It is truly a great testament to your faith and God's faithfulness!" His email was not full of the usual South American pleasantries, but was both direct and sincere. He continued, "As far as the container transportation costs are concerned, I would like to double what I offered before. Early tomorrow morning, I will transfer $10,000 to you!"

And the very next morning, the money was indeed in our account.

Since the first one in 2004, I have carefully logged the details of every presentation I have made: the location, the time, the number of participants, and the names of those who organized my visit. I have also noted any donations received.

Approximately 120,000 people in twenty-three countries on five continents have now heard my presentation. Pretty much all of them applauded, and many gave a one-time financial gift. Others, such as Hektor Dasso, committed larger donations. These decisions were not as a result of my "eloquence", but instead reflected what was in each person's heart at that time – their thoughts often unknown to me until much later.

GOD HAS SEEN US

Johannes Wilhelm is a good illustration of this. He is the manager of Ascobloc-Gastro, a German manufacturing company located in Dresden, which specializes in food service industry solutions. He generally presents with a rather flat persona – not someone who should quit his day job to go into the entertainment industry! I have met with him twice now; Michael Mörl probably twenty times. Herr Wilhelm is quiet, guarded, and withdrawn. When we asked him to donate kitchen equipment for the school, he slowly shook his head ambiguously. When we left his office that day, we had absolutely no idea what he intended to do. But when our container was packed for Peru, we discovered that Herr Wilhelm had donated eight appliances worth €20,000.

To be honest, he had responded in a very similar manner years earlier when we requested his support in setting up the hospital kitchen. For months he kept us wondering, then at virtually the last minute he had his team quickly pack up eight kitchen components worth €36,000, ready to make the transatlantic journey to Peru. He artfully calculated the actual cash value down to €6,000, then paid that price himself – not as the company manager but as a private individual. Great blessings often come from seemingly unlikely sources. The support we have received from Ascobloc-Gastro has been all the more appreciated perhaps because it was so often unforeseen.

Since we were planning to open the school in the coming March, we were really feeling the time crunch in the autumn of 2013. We simply had to have the buildings finished, ready to receive students. This was the responsibility of Udo Klemenz, but since the spring he had shared the task and his office with Johannes Bahr, an up-and-coming civil engineer from Regensburg. We all knew that the school would be Udo's last project with us. As Udo took Johannes under his wing, we hoped that the master builder would impart his wealth of knowledge to his new protégé.

In Peru, it often takes years for a new school to get an operating licence. We were advised to seek an agreement for the school to operate on a provisional basis until the official licence was granted. This turned out to be unnecessary, as a private school in Curahuasi was in the process of closing. Their licence was simply transferred to Diospi Suyana. As an additional benefit, we retained Nicolás Sierra Huarcaya in his role as Business Manager. Nicolás Sierra Huarcaya and Christian Bigalke would provide strong leadership for the Diospi Suyana school. We remain well aware that this unfolding of events was not of our doing, but that of Someone high above!

As 2013 rolled into 2014, Christian Bigalke arrived in Curahuasi with his family and began to pull his school team together. From January, the school office began accepting student registration packets. Social workers Carolin Klett and Julianna Rolli visited more than 200 homes in order to assess the living conditions and home situations of prospective pupils. The two marched along muddy paths, through wind and rain, from one hut to the next. The information they gleaned would help them to allocate financial assistance fairly, later on.

On 7 March 2014, Udo Klemenz provided the following report for the Diospi Suyana website: "Hello, Diospi Suyana Friends! The countdown rolls on relentlessly, and we are scheduled to open in just one week! Looking at the photos from just three weeks ago, I never would have dreamed we could make so much progress in such a short time – especially on the outdoor projects."

Diospi Suyana is always at its best under pressure. Construction workers and staff scurried across the building site like ants. In the midst of the madness, there was Burkhart Jochum, a carpenter from the Rhineland area who had constructed most of the hospital doors in 2007. When I phoned the Jochums in early 2014 to request his help, his wife responded that they had just been discussing that possibility earlier the same week!

Once that idea was set in motion, everything seemed to happen at once. Following a worship service in the Jochums' home church, someone gave him money for the flight to Peru. No sooner had he dropped his suitcase off in the apartment behind the hospital, his temporary home, Burkhart had the first board in hand to begin fashioning furniture.

On Thursday 13 March, we prepared for the school inauguration ceremony in the large gymnasium. We had hung a screen, projector, and LCD lamps on the walls and ceiling. Some 500 chairs and a number of benches provided seating for our anticipated audience of 800. Thirteen classrooms had been set up so beautifully that even school dropouts would surely be enticed to return. The workshop donated by WPU, the biology lab, and the computer centre testified to the quality of our facility – certainly on a par with that of Lima's most elite private schools. Even though the landscaping would take several more months to complete, the school would be open to students on Monday.

The ceremony was held the next day, 14 March. The programme was a full three hours of music, speeches, and multimedia presentations. My wife and I showed photos of our earlier work and expressed our future hope that the school would teach more than chemistry, physics, and maths, and provide a foundation of faith and perspective that transcends the grave.

In his address, headteacher Christian Bigalke placed the opening of the Diospi Suyana school within the context of Peruvian history, highlighting the disadvantage and discrimination certain social groups had experienced for centuries. With regard to other local schools, he expressed the desire for cooperation and partnership.

Representatives from the Ministry of Education commended our facility and educational model, stating that we were setting the standard for the whole of the Apurímac. The myriad flags displayed on stage underscored our international flair.

The teachers introduced themselves and their subject in a most entertaining fashion. It was clear that the staff were more eager to get started than perhaps even the students. Some had relocated to southern Peru specifically for the opportunity to teach at the Diospi Suyana school.

The audience gave Udo and Barbara Klemenz a well-deserved standing ovation for their excellent service in heading up construction of the school. I deemed them "living legends" and presented them with a wooden replica of a motorbike, symbolically encouraging them to use it to rush back to Curahuasi and help us with future projects.

Our tribute continued, to include the Linders' architectural firm, engineer Jürgen Engel, and a host of corporate and individual sponsors.

Speeches are usually heard, then quickly fade from memory. But when Damaris Huahuachampi sang the first note of the Diospi Suyana hymn, it was a moment not to be forgotten. Carolina Bochum had composed the music and penned the lyrics of this beloved hymn for the inauguration of the hospital back in 2007. The song speaks to the desperate situation of the Quechua people in the mountains of Peru, and the love of God made visible through Diospi Suyana.

23

Colégio Diospi Suyana

On Monday morning, 17 March 2014, we were greeted by 180 new students assembled in our school yard. Spruced up and lined up, their maroon jackets were on trend and coordinated perfectly with their grey trousers and skirts. Each item of the uniform, from socks to shirt collars, sported the official red-and-yellow Diospi Suyana logo.

Most of the children were Peruvians, their dark skin and black hair a tell-tale sign of their roots. Among them were lighter-skinned missionary children, making up approximately 10 per cent of the student body. The experiment of an international school that cut through ethnic and social strata had begun.

How such a diverse group could be unified into a cohesive student body was known to one person alone: Christian Bigalke. None of the Peruvian teachers had any knowledge of European or North American pedagogy, and we could only hope that their enthusiasm would not wane on the rough road of getting the school firmly established in the community. Our missionary team serving the school was quite varied in and of itself. We had Julianna Rolli from Hungary, Lilli Warkentin from Germany, and Alison Caire from the United States. These were later joined by Manuela Trinker from Austria and Damaris Brudy from Germany.

As the school term slowly got underway, construction and landscaping work was continuing outside. The students and labourers enjoyed a peaceful, enriching co-existence, with both groups joining together for the weekly school assemblies. Udo Klemenz demonstrated great consideration for the lessons, and did not allow the noise levels to rise until the school day had finished and the last student had gone home.

You can hope for success in a project, you can wish for it, you can even pray for it. But the one thing you cannot do is force it. Time would soon tell how Christian Bigalke would need to lead his team in order to keep them as optimistic and committed as they had been at the beginning. Some children in Year 5 were barely able to read and write. Scarcely literate, they had somehow made their way through their first few years of school – a rather damning reflection on the quality of the Peruvian educational system.

It wasn't long before the parents of some missionary students expressed concern. They had mistakenly assumed that Colégio Diospi Suyana would be similar in academic rigour to schools in Europe and North America. During an emergency meeting with all the missionary parents, Tina and I emphasized the benefits and potential of our school, expressing strong support for Christian and his team. Only patience, hard work, and time would raise the average level of achievement for such a mix of children, some of whom lived in the most heartbreaking conditions.

Take the example of Maria, a student in Year 2 who was growing up without a father. Her family's adobe hut had no running water. She and her two siblings ate breakfast sitting on their shared bed, for they did not own a table. Maria did not even know who her father was. Her mother had been raped while working as a housemaid in Lima. None of the

162

fathers of her siblings were present. Her mother struggled to support her family by working in the nearby fields.

Anderson, a boy in Year 4, was in a similar situation – living in a simple clay-brick house. His father was present, but was a raging alcoholic who frequently beat Anderson and his siblings until they were black and blue. His mother did not have steady work, but picked up odd jobs whenever she could.

The Colégio Diospi Suyana is a gift from heaven for children like Maria and Anderson. They get quality academic instruction, plus they learn self-discipline, punctuality, organization, and respect. But of much greater importance is the loving care they receive from their teachers. With absent or abusive fathers who do not take responsibility for bringing up their children, the teachers are faced with a tremendous task. At first they seek to establish a sense of trust with the children, then they look for ways to teach them their true value as children of God.

During the first year, Christian Bigalke and his team did a superb job in laying a firm foundation for subsequent years. Their task still is huge and the effort exhausting, but they draw their strength from their faith in God. They are not willing to passively accept the children's tragic circumstances as the status quo. They are actively and patiently working for productive change. In time, the Diospi Suyana school will bring about an enduring improvement in the Curahuasi area. Of that there is no doubt.

24

Who Foots the Bill?

Does running a hospital and a school cost money? You bet it does! And where does this money come from? Since the beginning of it all in 2004 up until April 2019, Diospi Suyana has received $30.6 million in goods and financial donations, not counting the financial support given directly to the missionaries themselves. That is an astronomical figure, very difficult to conceptualize. I will attempt to clarify the specifics of how we have stewarded all we have been so generously given.

The Diospi Suyana hospital was built and equipped with modern technology. The dental and eye clinics were also built and fitted with materials of the highest calibre. Our third project was the Kids' House for the Kids' Clubs. Now we have the school, with capacity for 700 students.

From October 2007 to April 2019, we treated 335,000 patients at the hospital. Approximately 1,000 patients required treatment in our intensive care unit. Our surgeons conducted more than 10,000 operations during this time period. Two thirds of these costs were covered by the Diospi Suyana Charitable Trust.

Week by week, our staff care for 400 children in the Kids' Clubs. There are currently 380 students enrolled in our school.

Our 200 Peruvian employees receive a monthly salary, and of course we contribute to their medical care and pension funds as well.

Then there are the everyday expenses – medication, plasters, vaccines, nails for the school workshop, and ink cartridges for the printers.

If you were to visit Diospi Suyana, you would see that everything is top quality – our facilities, our work, our level of care. This forces the question: "How can so much be accomplished with so little?" In the West, these projects and services would easily have cost ten times more.

The credit for our bookkeeping miracle belongs to God alone. Jesus once used five loaves and two fish to feed 5,000 people. At Diospi Suyana, we get by on the exact same principle. God moves people's hearts to support us financially. People give blood, sweat, and tears – quite literally. Almost a thousand individuals have made the commitment to support our work through regular giving. We would not exist but for their faithfulness.

So many fundraising events have been held on behalf of Diospi Suyana. Some probably should have earned a mention in the book of *Guinness World Records*. I will share some notable examples here.

Jörg and Swantje Böttger are a retired couple living in Schmachtenhagen, near Berlin. Once a month they invite people to a special dinner. They purchase all the ingredients themselves, then enjoy preparing the meal with friends. Usually they have about thirty guests gathered around their table. After the culinary delights have been thoroughly enjoyed, partakers donate to a fund earmarked for Diospi Suyana.

We can only imagine the work that goes into these evenings. And how many times have the Böttgers held these events? Maybe five times? Ten? By the end of March 2019, they had hosted 145 dinners in support of Diospi Suyana.

Jörg once said to me, "Klaus, I hope we can do a hundred of these meals."

I responded, "Jörg, why not *two* hundred?"

My mother always said I had cheek. Now you know why!

Christine Fleck, from Kirchheimbolanden, wrote to me several years ago about her marvellous idea to sell packets of home-made granola to raise money for Diospi Suyana. When I first read this, I wasn't sure about it. Clearly I had not spent enough time in the kitchen, and had seriously underestimated the power of granola. By the spring of 2019, Christine had earned more than €65,000 for Diospi Suyana, right from her own kitchen. A sturdy baking pan and a high degree of stamina were necessary to make this happen. With this kind of dedication and energy, Christine could compete in the Ironman challenge and win!

Since 2004, we have sent out a printed newsletter highlighting progress in our work and specific projects five times each year. At the time of writing, sixty-nine editions of our newsletter have been published. Occasionally, supporters will ask to receive the newsletter via email in order to keep our costs down. But we keep on with the printed version for several important reasons.

The printers Klaus Koch supplied the high-quality paper and printed all of our newsletters at their own expense. I am familiar with quite a few printing companies and I understand it is an extremely competitive industry. Owning a printing company does not translate to having an easy life! But Andreas and Matthias Koch have chosen to support the work of Diospi Suyana in this generous manner for more than a decade. Addressing the envelopes is done many times by a team of volunteers. By the time they get to the 10,000th envelope, they are about ready to collapse from exhaustion.

The Diospi Suyana newsletters can be found on many a coffee table, stuck to refrigerators, or available as reading material in the WC. One copy may be read by every member of a household, then passed along to the next-door neighbour. An email just doesn't get the same kind of circulation! With many thanks to the Koch family, we will continue to utilize Johannes Gutenberg's priceless invention for our newsletter.

Have you seen the Diospi Suyana brochures? The logo is bright red, and the background a tasteful, neutral beige. In 2004, graphic artist Bernd Schermuly designed our corporate logo. He has a sophisticated understanding of space and colour. With his simple but bold design, I feel he truly captured the essence of who we are.

In 2013, Bernd substantially upgraded our website. After a hundred hours of labour, he had completed his "magnum opus". He did not request or receive any payment for this massive effort. He personally purchased multiple software programs so that they could be integrated on our webpages. He monitors the use of the site and can spot a potential hacker before damage can be done. What he has given to Diospi Suyana, via time and materials, easily totals at least five figures in monetary value.

German student Agnes Kloft organized a benefit concert on behalf of Diospi Suyana at her school in Stockholm. Organist Michael Raithelhuber performed an organ recital at St Mary's Church in Stuttgart, with all the proceeds going to Diospi Suyana. In Reutlingen, the band anna mo used their musical gifts to raise €2,000, and Italian vocalist Sefora Nelson sang her way into the hearts of her audience in Wuppertal, all for the benefit of Diospi Suyana. The Free Christian School in Frankfurt has also sponsored a fundraising concert on our behalf. Over the years, musicians of all varieties have graciously given of their time and talent to raise financial support and awareness of the Diospi Suyana cause.

Head girl Lisa Höfler had a thousand fellow pupils at Burkstädt Grammar School sweating as she organized a fundraising run. All the participants viewed the Diospi Suyana film prior to the start, just to keep them motivated all the way to the finish line. In Gelnhausen, eighty-five runners from the Protestant Church of the Nazarene collectively managed 1,527 total laps around an athletic track, raising more than €4,000.

Some people burn calories to help us, others consume them in delicious creations baked for the same cause! Numerous bake sales have been held over the years. The Catholic Kolping Society of Celle even slaughtered a couple of pigs and rang the church bells as musical accompaniment for the meal!

Largely owing to these fundraisers, Diospi Suyana has never had to turn away a patient in need, regardless of his or her ability to pay. Our passionate friends have not only achieved incredible financial results, but their spirit and their efforts have also encouraged us to keep going even in the face of adversity.

This kind of passion also inspired theologian Markus Wehrstedt, astrophysicist Michael Wehrstedt, and administrative assistant Angelika Brünger to establish the Encourager Foundation. Since 2005, they have provided us with regular funding support.

Donations given in honour of loved ones on birthdays, weddings, anniversaries, and in memoriam have contributed

GOD HAS SEEN US

significantly to the construction and implementation of our various projects. We cannot thank our supporters enough for all they have done. And we are sure that even the least that is given, God will multiply and use for His glory and purpose.

25

Commissioned at Dawn

Some people enthusiastically present new ideas, many of them worthwhile, but without the stamina and drive to follow through to a clearly defined goal, these ideas fizzle out and die. People move on to the next idea. Just a flash in the pan. All talk, no real action. A waste.

Walter Enders, however, is a man of quite a different calibre. Hailing from Saxony, Walter has made a profound impression upon me over the many years I have known him. For fifteen years, he served as the caretaker of a church in Wiesbaden, a perfect position for someone as conscientious and responsible as he is. This man has both feet firmly planted on solid ground. He enjoys many blessings in this life. One of the blessings he appears to enjoy the most is that of sleep. The man likes his sleep. He opens his eyes as soon as the alarm goes off each morning, but not a minute before.

Things were a little different on 20 July 2005 – a Wednesday he has never forgotten, even though it was more than ten years ago.

At 5 a.m. Walter woke up. He heard God speak to him in a still, small voice, clearly instructing him to get a glass jar (the type with a flip lid and lock, usually used for preserving food), to cut a slit into the lid, and to write on the jar: "For the work of faith in Peru. God thanks you for every cent so that the hospital might grow and thrive." In his mind's eye, Walter

170

could see the jar, prepared as he had just been directed in detail by God himself.

By 7 a.m. Walter was at the church. He found a jar and attempted to cut a slit into the lid. Pieces of shattered glass flew everywhere. This wasn't going to work. Had he misheard the very particular instructions? Had he dreamed it all? No, God had given him a specific job to do – Walter was certain.

A little later, our caretaker went into a small houseware shop.

"I need some jars with flip lids. Do you have some in stock?" he asked.

The salesman shook his head. "No, I'm sorry. I don't have any in the shop or the warehouse. Shall I order some for you?"

Another customer overheard the conversation and chimed in: "I've just seen what you're looking for in Walmart. They're on special offer – just a little over €2 each!"

Walter Enders found the exact jars there and took them to a glazier to have the slits properly cut into the lids. The first one told him that what he was asking could not be done. The second one said the same thing. So did the third! The fourth suggested yet another glazier in Mainz who might be able to help.

So Walter drove over the bridge into the Rhineland-Palatinate and headed straight to Glasbau Mainz GmbH. When he told an employee what he wanted, the man shrugged.

"I can't guarantee that it will work, but if that is what you want, I can try with this special cutting machine."

Just seconds later, a perfect slit was right where it needed to be, and the jar was transformed into a see-through piggybank.

Since 2005, we have had more than sixty of these jars out in shops, doctors' surgeries, pharmacies, and even hair salons. Patrons of these establishments frequently contribute coins received as change after paying their bill. At the time of writing, more than €15,000 has been donated to Diospi Suyana in this manner. A little jar, a little change – a big difference to Diospi Suyana!

Walter Enders heard God speak to him that morning. It was unexpected but unmistakable. My wife and I were just preparing to leave for Peru to start the massive Diospi Suyana project when this happened. Walter's actions were a great encouragement to us then, and remain so today. It's all just another example of how God moves in mysterious ways, and perhaps when we least expect it. As the old Boy Scout motto exhorts, we should always "Be Prepared"!

26

Helicopter from Heaven

By midnight on 6 June 2011, the outcome of the Peruvian presidential election was becoming clear. By morning, it was absolutely certain. Ollanta Humala was the new president of Peru. The lieutenant colonel had managed to defeat Keiko Fujimori, the daughter of the former dictator Alberto Fujimori. Keiko Fujimori had been slightly ahead in the polls just a week earlier, but a portentous shift occurred in the days immediately prior to the election. She received a disappointing 48.5 per cent of the vote.

My wife and I digested this news with unease. Ollanta Humala had quite a history. He was the one who had led the attempted coup against President Fujimori back in 2000. His brother Antauro was serving time in prison for his role in a different rebellion, and his father Isaac was known as one of the founders of a radical ethnic nationalist party. The media used tough language when referring to the Humala family. Would the new power in the presidential palace see fit to deport all foreigners and take over their companies? On television, he had placed his left hand on a Bible and sworn to uphold the constitution of his country. But was such a gesture worth anything from a man who claimed no faith? Might our mission hospital end up in the crosshairs of his militant political allies? Over the course of history, hundreds of mission hospitals all over the world have been nationalized

GOD HAS SEEN US

or forced to close at the whim of merciless government authorities.

It was clear to me that we would need to reach out to the newly elected president and First Lady. Establishing a positive relationship would be the best way for us to respond to the current political change. But how could we go about this? I did not know anyone close to him, and in terms of our worldview, we were clearly miles apart. Still, we needed to try. I knew well that God could open even the most tightly shut door.

I had first made an overture towards Ollanta and his wife, Nadine Heredia, during the election campaign. On 15 April 2011, we welcomed a delegation from ADIFAN, a fifteen-company pharmaceutical conglomerate that intended to donate $50,000 of medication to Diospi Suyana. The head of ADIFAN, along with two other executives, wished to present the boxes of medication during a formal ceremony following our hospital chapel service one morning.

Luis Caballeros' speech in the crowded chapel that day was memorable in several respects. He saw the poor patients sitting right in front of him, and realized perhaps for the first time what Diospi Suyana meant for thousands of forgotten and hopeless people in the mountains. I can only imagine what was going through his mind as he stood at the lectern, struggling for words, the tears streaming freely down his face.

Once he had more or less collected himself, Luis Caballeros shared the story of his first acquaintance with Diospi Suyana as the audience held their breath in rapt anticipation. One morning, he had simply encountered a bound collection of Diospi Suyana photos with the title "The

Hospital of Faith" printed on the red cover. The book was on his desk, and to this day he has no idea how it got there. But the photographs most certainly touched his heart.

I sat in the front row of the chapel, nodding. I was familiar with this story. Shortly after reading the volume (2,000 copies of which the Peruvian company Neptunia had given to us as a donation), he invited me to his office, where I shared the story of Diospi Suyana with him in person.

Patients and staff all saw that morning that Luis Caballeros was completely captivated by the work of Diospi Suyana. A tour of our various hospital departments only intensified his great esteem for our mission.

That evening, he and two colleagues sat at our dining room table, enjoying soup and a main course from my wife's impressive culinary repertoire. Naturally, we discussed recent political developments and speculated on the outcome of the upcoming election.

"The day after tomorrow, Ollanta Humala and Nadine will be visiting ADIFAN," Señor Caballeros shared proudly. "I could extend an invitation on behalf of Diospi Suyana while they are there."

That sentence was enough to grab my attention away from the lasagne on the table before me.

"Would you really do that for us?" I asked breathlessly.

"Without a doubt," our guest assured me, looking rather pleased. "It would be a great honour for me to be able to help you."

Luis Caballeros kept his word. My invitation, accompanied by lots of colour photos and a few newspaper articles, was in fact delivered to the intended recipient.

But there was no response.

Nearly two years later, at approximately 10 o'clock on the morning of 25 April 2013, I entered the German ambassador's office. I visit the German embassy regularly to keep the diplomat apprised of our activities. I had expressed much gratitude to Joachim Christoph Schmelling for his support in getting container 32 released from customs three months previously, but he now greeted me quite coldly. In our most recent newsletter, I had attributed the release of the container to the prayerful intercession of friends all over the world. This was not a view that Herr Schmelling shared.

Visibly annoyed, Herr Schmelling abruptly declared, "It was not God but the German embassy who helped you!"

The harshness of his tone was startling. In the very brief conversation that followed, Herr Schmelling made it clear that in his mind God did not exist. Therefore logic dictated that someone who did not exist simply could not act.

In retrospect, I probably should have excused myself soon after that exchange. When there is such tension, it is best not to broach new topics or make requests. But instead I ploughed on, choosing to ignore the strained atmosphere. I would never have made a good politician.

"Your Excellency," I began, with the greatest tone of respect I could muster at that moment, "could you perhaps bring your influence to bear and arrange an audience with the First Lady? My wife and I would be exceedingly grateful for the opportunity to speak with her."

"No, I won't," Herr Schmelling retorted. "It is extremely difficult to get an appointment with her. There are lots of people who would like to speak to her. If I helped you, I would have to help everybody."

I registered the dismissive look on the ambassador's face and held my tongue. Dejectedly, I knew it was time to leave. But before I did, the ambassador got in one last word.

"Dr John, a meeting with the president or First Lady would be highly unlikely!" he repeated severely.

At that exact moment, I had a sense of déjà vu. I recalled the summer of 2006, when the German ambassador at that time, Dr Kliesow, had assured me that my desire for an audience with First Lady Pilar Nores was completely preposterous and that he would never exert his influence on behalf of such a brazen request. And yet, just one month later, my wife and I were personally received by the wife of President Alan García.

I took heart. If Ambassador Schmelling thought that Nadine Heredia would not give "Little Klaus John" a few minutes of her precious time, then the stage was perfectly set for God to intervene in a seemingly "impossible" situation. A turnaround would perhaps be even more dramatic since Herr Schmelling had already discounted God.

On 21 June 2013, I was much closer to my goal. Congressman Jesus Hurtado arranged for me to meet with Ana Jara, the Minister for Women and Vulnerable Populations. She was a member of the same political party as the president, but, more significantly, she was personally close to First Lady Nadine Heredia. Ana Jara battled fatigue as I shared the story of Diospi Suyana with her and the Vice Minister that evening. I occasionally had to raise my voice during my presentation to rouse her when she nodded off.

"How can I help you?" Ana Jara asked with South American courtesy at the conclusion of my presentation.

I didn't need to think long before answering, as I had not flown to Lima just for the joy of spending forty-five minutes in her presence.

"I would be grateful if you could please arrange an opportunity for me to meet with the president's wife."

Ana Jara grasped the significance of my request. Charities, in particular, need the support of the president and his wife. Difficulties importing donated goods and conflicts with local authorities are often only resolved through the intervention of important members of the political and/or economic sectors.

"OK, I will use my influence on your behalf," the Minister promised me. Wanting to help us further, she added, "If I could give you one small piece of advice, though. You might want to remove any photos of former presidents from your presentation!"

Walking out into the cool evening, I inhaled deeply. My plan seemed to be working. But then days went by and turned into weeks. Weeks turned into months. And still the anticipated email from the Minister never arrived. After six long months, I concluded that Ana Jara had quite simply forgotten about me.

Every now and then I would encounter a photo of the president and his wife in a magazine, and sigh out loud. Ollanta Humala and Nadine Heredia remained out of reach. The distance was so much greater than the actual mileage between Lima and Curahuasi.

Exhausted, I got off the plane in Cusco on 28 May 2014. My three weeks of touring through England, Spain, and Germany were finally over. I had shared the story of Diospi Suyana as often as possible along the way, and was now completely drained. I was glad that my wife would be able to pick me up from the airport, and that we would be together for the two-and-a-half-hour drive home.

GOD HAS SEEN US

Tina was carefully manoeuvring our car along the highway from Cusco when my phone rang. I picked up and had Stefan Seiler from our administration department on the line.

"Just wanted to let you know that the president will be landing on our helicopter pad the day after tomorrow!"

"Really?" I asked, somewhat sceptically.

Peru is a place rife with rumours. Fantastic stories more often than not turn out to be wishful thinking or someone's bid for attention or importance. But Stefan seemed pretty sure of himself.

"Yes, the president really is coming. His security detail is inspecting our helipad as we speak!"

The next morning, I had a meeting scheduled with the mayor of Curahuasi, Guillermo Vergara, regarding a different matter. I asked for his input on a possible visit by the president. Mayor Vergara's eyes sparkled with excitement as he drew me into the intricacies of politics. Not just the president but his entire cabinet would be landing in Curahuasi in less than twenty-four hours. They would arrive in three helicopters, and the one carrying the president himself would land in a nearby stadium. The officials would spend the entire day in and around the Curahuasi town hall, meeting with mayors from cities across the region of Apurímac. Why the president wanted to hold such a gathering in the remote town of Curahuasi, the mayor did not say.

I was disappointed. I walked down the steps from the mayor's third-floor office. It looked as though we would just miss having contact with the president. Protocol had thrown a spanner in the works. I sighed. If only his helicopter could land on our helipad rather than in the stadium, we would be able to welcome him and perhaps divert him for a quick tour through our hospital. If only…. If only…. But as a child I had been taught the axiom that we were not to live in "If Only Land".

Far into the night, officials from Lima and town hall staff met to sort out the summit details with military precision. Agustin Landeras, head of our logistics department, joined them at the table and did his best to exert some influence on the planning.

Lo and behold, when I arrived at the hospital at 7:30 on Friday morning, I learned that there had been a change of plan. The president's personal assistant, Maria Elena Juscamaita, informed me that the president would be landing on our helipad after all, but would need to be driven straight from there to the centre of town in order to speak to the residents.

"Señora," I beseeched, "we would really like to offer the president a short tour of our hospital before he leaves. May I show you, quickly?"

Less than five minutes later, we were standing at the front of the hospital reception area. Señora Juscamaita was impressed.

"You are providing a wonderful service for the poor of our country. It would be so good if our president could see this for himself."

I certainly hadn't expected that reaction, but what she said next was positively mind-blowing.

"I have known of you and your wife since 2009," the president's personal assistant explained. "When you applied for honorary citizenship, I worked on your case and signed off on it. I have the greatest respect for your mission."

With these words she handed me her business card with contact details at the presidential palace. For three long years I had lamented our lack of access to the president, and now I was learning that his personal assistant thought very highly of us. I held on tight to the card with her telephone number and email address.

After the morning chapel service, I invited several staff members into my office to pray. None of us knew what the coming hours would bring, but we wanted to ask God for His blessing and guidance. As the last "amen" was voiced, we stood up, stronger and more mentally prepared after praying together. No matter what happened today, we could be confident that God held it all safe in His hands.

The president was due to land at 10:30 a.m. Members of the hospital staff, his security detail, and curious bystanders were beginning to congregate near the helipad about an hour before the expected arrival. Udo Klemenz rather astutely positioned himself right next to me. After all, as our leading civil engineer, the beautifully round landing pad was his work. There may not have been many landings on this helipad, but there was about to be an extremely significant one.

Two cars drove up to the hospital. The mayor and his advisors climbed out of the first vehicle, the president of the Apurímac region, Elias Segovia, out of the second. We exchanged pleasantries and I explained my plan to them while we waited for the Head of State's arrival. We intended to invite him on a quick detour through the hospital. Inside, we had more than a hundred patients from – as I had learned that morning – eight different regions of Peru. Nobody objected to my suggestion until the president's chief protocol officer rounded the corner.

GOD HAS SEEN US

"Dr John, please be aware that the president will not be coming into your hospital!" Señor Haya sounded very annoyed. "The president's departure from Andahuaylas has been delayed by almost ninety minutes. As soon as he lands, he must go straight to Plaza de Armas."

Discouraged, I approached the mayor, who was deep in conversation with two security officers.

"Señor Mayor," I whispered, "Señor Haya doesn't want the president to come into our hospital – he said the schedule is too tight."

Guillermo Vergara showed no signs of concern, saying, "Dr John, have a bit more faith!" The town politician reminding the missionary doctor that all things are possible with God – the irony was kind of funny.

"Let's hope for the best," I replied doubtfully, looking the mayor in the eye.

At noon, we finally heard the whirring of a helicopter in the distance. The sun beat down mercilessly as we waited. The ninety-minute delay Señor Haya had reported was sadly true, and the inevitable cost was that there would be no time for anything other than a quick handshake.

The helicopter made its approach, circled the site, then touched down with a deafening roar in the middle of our helipad. Two reporters from the regional Channel 7 jumped out of the helicopter first so they could capture the president's arrival on camera. Then we saw Ollanta Humala himself striding towards us, wearing a bright red poncho.

After the elected officials had greeted their leader, it was our turn. My wife Tina and I, then Stefan Seiler, Udo Klemenz, and Christian Bigalke, our headteacher, all shook the president's hand.

"Señor President," I began with little hope, "it would be a great honour for us to be able to accompany you into the hospital reception area for just a few minutes."

I had reluctantly succumbed to reality and reduced my original hopes of a hospital tour to just a quick peek into the entrance area.

Ollanta Humala flashed a friendly smile. "I have to go straight to the plaza," he said. "The ministers are waiting for me there."

I nodded imperceptibly. Of course, he was right.

"But I have read about your hospital in a magazine," he continued. "Perhaps there will be time before my return flight this afternoon for a quick tour."

Brilliant! That was our solution then. The hope that seldom leaves me was renewed. We had a window of five hours before the president would need to depart.

The town hall was bustling with a large group of local politicians gathering outside, while inside the president was in session with his ministers and invited guests.

Meanwhile, from 4 p.m., our staff gathered in front of the hospital in sight of the helicopter. I had asked Lisa Isaak and Sarah Nafziger to take photos of every move the president made during his visit to Diospi Suyana, preserving the historic event for all eternity. Ryan Morigeau would do his very best to produce top-quality video clips.

I grew increasingly unsettled, glancing at my watch every few seconds. The president's helicopter had to take off by 5 p.m. at the latest in order to get him to Cusco safely and on time for his flight back to the capital. This was a schedule determined less by protocol and more by the onset of darkness at 5:30 p.m. I might have been able to negotiate with the president's staff, but I was powerless to halt the setting of the sun.

Time continued to pass. Perspiration ran down my spine. I phoned the town hall every few minutes for a status update. My contacts there reported the same thing each time: "The final document is being read aloud, then the president needs to sign it. We will call you as soon as he leaves the town hall!"

The big hand of the clock was getting dangerously close to the twelve. It was looking as if we had lost our race against time.

Then I heard members of staff crying out excitedly, "He's coming!" Within seconds we were all in motion.

Ollanta Humala was driving the pick-up truck himself, three of his bodyguards hanging tightly to the pole across the flatbed. We waved the president directly to the hospital entrance.

"Señor President, how much time do you have?" I asked, getting straight to the point.

"Maybe ten minutes," he answered.

"Right, then, let's get moving!"

It is difficult to describe the scene that unfolded over the next fifteen minutes. Ollanta Humala and I hurried down the corridor, with about a hundred people scurrying behind us, trying to keep up. My descriptions of the various departments were reduced to isolated words rather than comprehensive sentences. There was nothing "presidential" about this whirlwind tour. We were just humans on a potentially impossible mission: that of winning over the heart of the Head of State.

The atmosphere resembled that of a party more than an official state visit. There were smiling faces everywhere. We were having a blast, President Humala smiling among us all. He really seemed to be enjoying this mad dash through the hospital corridors. The tension of the previous hours, weighed down by protocol and the expectations of his constituents, just melted off him. For a few minutes, the president, the missionaries, and the rest of the hospital staff became brothers in the truest sense of the word.

It was ten past five. The last photos were snapped as a radiant president stood surrounded by delighted people at the hospital entrance. He and I then ran together towards the helipad.

"You're in better shape than I am!" I praised the man running alongside me.

"What do you need for your hospital?" the president called out to me.

I was ready with my answer: "An audience with you and your wife at the presidential palace!"

The president laughed and essentially responded with a "thumbs up". He jumped down the steps to the helipad. The helicopter took off, heading for Cusco.

Wanting to end the day as we had started it, we gathered around a table in my office. Prayers of thanksgiving poured from the depths of our hearts. None of us could adequately explain the events of the last twenty minutes. We had witnessed it with our own eyes, yet it felt like a dream – a wonderful dream. But we knew that God, the original Great Chemist, had mixed all the right elements in the flasks – the chemistry between Ollanta Humala and us had been perfect.

Just after 7 p.m. that same evening, my phone rang. It was the mayor, and I had never heard him so excited.

"Dr John, the president just rang me from Lima. He's absolutely fascinated by the Diospi Suyana hospital. He said it's the best in the whole of southern Peru!"

GOD HAS SEEN US

Six days later, on 5 June 2014, my wife and I, accompanied by Dr Jens Hassfeld, crossed the threshold of the presidential palace. We were led into an elegantly panelled conference room. In no time at all I had my laptop set up and connected to the giant presentation display screen.

The three of us stared in anticipation at the wooden door. The door opened, the president and his wife entered, and they greeted us warmly.

My presentation covered the story of Diospi Suyana in about 120 slides. Peru had become our new home so that we can show the love of Christ to the Quechua people. As always, at the end of the presentation, I showed the cross of Christ, identifying it as the motive for our work, and the empty tomb, identifying it as our source of hope.

I had tried my best to get an audience with the president for three whole years, to no avail. But at the end of the day, the president had come to me: his helicopter landed on my helipad and he asked me what was needed for the hospital. When I said I needed an audience with him, he responded, "No problem!"

On Saturday afternoon, 7 September 2014, I was driving north on an English motorway, heading to the first of my scheduled public presentations in Great Britain, which would take place the following day. My mobile rang and I noted a strange number on the display. It was an employee of the presidential palace in Lima.

"Dr John, the president has a niece in Switzerland," he explained matter-of-factly. "She would like to volunteer at your hospital for a few months."

I asked the official to send me her contact information. A few days later, we exchanged emails, followed by a personal phone call. Carol Seiffert was a newly qualified dentist – as well as the niece of the president of Peru. She told me that her uncle and aunt, the president and First Lady, had warmly recommended the Diospi Suyana hospital.

On 8 October 2014, Carol flew to Lima and stayed with her grandparents, the president's parents, in the capital for a few days. When the Peruvian Congress awarded my wife and me certificates of honour for our life's work on 10 October, we had three guests of honour in the front row: Carol Seiffert with her grandmother and grandfather.

In the Bible it says that with God's help we can scale walls. Lack of time, differences in social status, political and religious ideologies all lose their divisive power in the hands of God. If God wills it, then the president will fly straight to our doorstep, shake our hands, and invite us to his palace.

And that is the story of how I met the president of Peru, his wife, his sister from Switzerland, his niece, and his parents – all in person.

27

The Power of Print

A considerable number of people wish they had recorded the story of their lives for posterity. Unfortunately, when this regret comes on one's deathbed, it is too late to do much about it. I experienced this same feeling of remorse on 16 December 2008, when I stood on the edge of a mountain precipice, having been injured in a serious car crash. In that very dark and frightening moment, my first thoughts were of the autobiography I had never got around to writing – a situation quickly remedied in the first half of 2009.

My 272-page manuscript was published by Brunnen, a Christian publishing house based in Germany, in March 2010. Within days, I was astounded by the effect one book can have. It was recognized on the radio and TV, and covered extensively in the press. By the spring of 2019, almost 42,000 copies, representing nine editions, had been sold!

My wife and I donate the proceeds of the book to various humanitarian projects in Africa, the Middle East, and South America. Although we are the authors of the book, the story is God's blessing alone, and we do not wish to profit monetarily. Truly, we have been more than well "paid" by the overwhelming response of our readers.

Many readers have gone to work with a pounding headache because they unwisely picked up the book right before bedtime – then found themselves unable to put it down! By dawn, they reached the last page, then had to drag themselves out of bed, taking on the new day with little or no sleep.

Literally thousands of our readers have made very generous financial donations to Diospi Suyana after finishing the book, regardless of whether they share our Christian faith. To date, nearly fifty tradespeople and academics have relinquished jobs in their home countries in order to serve long term as unsalaried missionaries at the Diospi Suyana hospital – a decision they made after reading the book.

On average, one in every hundred readers contacts our German office, sharing often very personal testimony of how the story has moved them.

Peter H., from the Netherlands, wrote and told us that his daughter had picked up a copy of our book at Heathrow Airport in London, then passed it along to him. He had read a chapter a day on his journey to work each morning. Since then, he has resumed praying – a habit he had dropped some time before. He is now praying in particular for members of his family.

In a Benedictine monastery in Fischingen, Switzerland, one monk read my book aloud, from cover to cover, to all the brothers during mealtimes. They recognized God's power at work in Diospi Suyana, and their own faith was strengthened as a result.

After reading *I Have Seen God*, Margot Steiner and Christa Meandzija were convinced that God could indeed do all things. They opened a Christian bookshop in Krems, Austria, believing that the challenges of operating such a shop in a secular society would be no problem at all for God.

Maria Meister, from the Rhine-Main area of Germany, may have had trouble seeing at her advanced age of ninety-one years, but that didn't stop her from reading the entire book with a magnifying glass! She personally attended one of my presentations in Mainz, and it was my privilege to sign her copy of my book.

One day, Austrian Franz Forster discovered a Diospi Suyana brochure in his flat. Curious, he looked us up on the internet. Further intrigued by what he read there, he ordered the book – and became completely hooked. A Catholic believer himself, Franz felt that more people should be able to read this story. The Forsters purchased ten more copies of *I Have Seen God*, lending them freely to friends and family. As soon as one copy was returned, it was passed along to someone else. Their private "lending library" flourished for months – even though it only stocked one title!

Teacher Wolfgang M. was given a copy of the book by a colleague. A few weeks later, he sent her the following email:

> *First of all, I must admit that God, church, and faith are not really my cup of tea, so initially I wasn't overly interested in this book. For the past few weeks, my son has been doing a swimming course at the weekends. I grabbed a book to read while I was waiting for him – it just happened to be the one you gave me. I started to flip through it – quite sceptically at first. But then I really got into it, and finished it in a short period of time, probably because it is written in such an entertaining manner. The "miracles" that Dr John experienced could easily be dismissed as coincidence, but maybe there really is this higher power. Maybe it was this same higher power that made me take the book to the swimming lessons!*

190

A professor of paediatric surgery from Tübingen devoured the book, then started going back to church after many years away. He wrote, "I didn't even know the preacher, but he gave a very good sermon on the highs and lows in life, and the events or miracles that amaze us. I couldn't help but think of you and Diospi Suyana!"

Time and time again, my wife and I have been deeply moved by the response of our readers. It was no surprise that on 30 July 2010 I was hit with sudden inspiration. I was sitting at my desk in the hospital. On my computer screen was an email from a lady regarding my "Encourager Book", as she termed it. I started to ponder a possibility: wouldn't it be a good idea to make this story available to English-speaking readers as well?

My thoughts turned to Janet Yachoua, a friendly English lady who had been living in Wiesbaden for thirty years and ran her own translation business. Over the years, she had already translated quite a bit of text for the English version of our website. I sent her a carefully worded email across the Atlantic, asking her two questions. First of all, had she heard of the book? And second, would she be willing to help with the translation?

You could have knocked me over with a feather when her reply came the very next day: "Believe it or not, I was just thinking yesterday about translating the book, and I spent some time praying for you... a couple of hours later, you emailed me – it sounds like a divine plan! When do you need it?"

I had not had much contact with Janet over the previous two years, but she was familiar with the book. In fact, it had been sitting on her desk all summer. At the exact moment

I was typing my email to her, she was standing in front of her desk, thousands of miles away, looking at the book and experiencing an inner call to translate it.

So what do you think Janet Yachoua did? Over the next few months, she painstakingly translated the entire text, word for word, into English. This English version became the basis for the Spanish version, published in 2011, and a youth edition, published in several languages in 2012. In 2014, the English publisher Lion Hudson made *I Have Seen God* available to the entire English-speaking world. In 2015, a Romanian translation was published, also using the English version as its base.

Janet did not accept a single penny for this monumental task.

My book has engaged many a reader snuggled in bed or lounging on a sunny beach. I am happy about this, of course, but when I wrote it, I intended it to be so much more than "entertainment". What I really wanted was to "shout from the rooftops" that I had first-hand experience and evidence in my life to support the reality of God. I am not the only one who thinks so. Peru's leading newspaper, *El Comercio*, wrote in the 22 July 2007 edition, "It is impossible not to believe in miracles when you hear the story of Klaus John and his family!"

Perhaps this would be an appropriate time to consider what a miracle actually is. If the weather report forecasts rain for the next day, and in actuality the sun shines, that is a pleasant surprise for tourists (maybe not so much for farmers), but it is definitely not a miracle.

If after many years you suddenly run into an old classmate on the New York subway, that is unexpected and remarkable.

But if you try to pass it off as a miracle, a sceptic will merely regard you with disdain.

Diospi Suyana, however, is a different matter. It is one of the most modern hospitals in Peru, built in record time, without any debts or loans, and without a rich patron to drop millions of dollars into our account. Over the course of several years, my wife and I were led from one inexplicable episode to another. These "coincidences" and acts of providence were sequential, all leading in the same direction. A judge in Dillenburg came to a very telling conclusion following one of my presentations. He said that if a court needed to determine whether God existed based on circumstantial evidence, what I had experienced would be sufficient for a favourable ruling.

On 6 May 2014, John Lennox granted me a two-hour appointment. Professor Emeritus of Mathematics at Oxford University, and a Fellow in Mathematics and the Philosophy of Science at Green Templeton College in Oxford, Dr Lennox is also an internationally renowned Christian apologist. His public debates with atheist Richard Dawkins have been viewed by millions via television and YouTube. He has also contended with Christopher Hitchens, Victor Stenger, and Michael Shermer – all leading proponents of an atheistic worldview. His book, *God's Undertaker*, may be considered the supreme rebuttal of atheist publications such as Dawkins' *The God Delusion*.

It was the first time Dr Lennox had heard of the "Hospital of Faith" in Peru. As I shared my presentation, my German accent did not seem to cause Dr Lennox any inconvenience – but, of course, this professor from Northern Ireland speaks fluent German, English, French, Russian, and Spanish!

A few weeks later, Dr Lennox wrote a review of my book, the words of which I will rejoice over until the end of my days:

> *As a scientist I am very interested in evidence from a study of the cosmos that supports the existence of God. But I am not just a theist, I am a Christian. One of the central tenets of the Christian faith is that we can have a personal relationship with God through Jesus Christ. It therefore follows that the credibility of the Christian faith can also be examined by testing this very claim regarding a personal God in daily life. The story of the Diospi Suyana hospital is a remarkable example of what can happen when people take God seriously. I heartily recommend this account as compelling evidence that there is a God who cares.*

GOD HAS SEEN US

28

Shrieking in A & E

The ongoing battle between Good and Evil is a popular theme in Hollywood. In westerns, the hero with the revolver prevails against a group of outlaws. Ben Hur wins his legendary chariot race against the two-faced Messala. Agent 007 escapes from the clutches of underworld enemies at the last possible moment.

At Diospi Suyana we also battle against evil. Indifferent and corrupt politicians complicate our lives. Anonymous individuals who are envious of our work seek to destroy our reputation through lies and accusations. We are a thorn in the side of those who sell liquor, for while they are lining their pockets with profits at the expense of their customers' health, we are actively combating the effects of alcoholism and seeking to mitigate the causes through our work at the hospital and Kids' Clubs.

On top of this, we see characteristics in our own selves that are neither noble nor admirable. We have our "dark sides" that perhaps we seek to excuse as a result of a difficult childhood, unfavourable circumstances, or other negative influences that are not our fault. Christians believe that God is good, and all that is good comes from Him. But the Bible goes on to affirm that there is evil in the world, malevolent powers that seek to confound God's people through lies and temptation.

Maybe you are raising an eyebrow right now. Maybe words such as "fairy tale" are crossing your mind. I can honestly understand your scepticism. But even agnostics start to question their convictions when they see the butchery in Rwanda displayed on their television screens. People who used to be peaceable neighbours suddenly reach for their knives and slit each other's throats. Such senseless cruelty is not confined to far-away places, such as Africa, but is clear to see in German history as well. This nation that produced brilliant poets, philosophers, and composers was suddenly capable of deporting, torturing, and murdering as many as 7 million Jews. To accomplish this magnitude of evil, it takes more than just a Hitler, a Himmler, and a Goebbels. Thousands upon thousands of German citizens were complicit, out of either "duty" or fear. They served as guards, train engineers, and the like – ultimately supporting this heinous genocide.

Around midday on 12 December 2012, I placed a quick call to my wife. I had just given a presentation to the Congressional Committee on Health, and members had responded very positively, regardless of their individual political affiliations. They were even inspired to award Martina and me a Congressional Medal of Honour!

But what Martina shared with me on the phone that day made my news pale into insignificance. There had been an incident at the hospital that morning while I was away. In the days following, I spoke to many eyewitnesses and have attempted to compile as detailed a report as possible. Make of it what you will.

At approximately 10 a.m. a taxi pulled up to the main entrance of the Diospi Suyana hospital. The three passengers, a mother and her two daughters from the town of Abancay, entered the waiting area and looked for available seats.

The *Jesus* film was showing that day, as every day, on the giant flat-screen TV at the front of the waiting area. Released some thirty years ago, the *Jesus* film is the most effective film project of all time. Translated into more than a thousand languages, it depicts the life of Jesus from birth to ascension, as presented in the New Testament Gospel of Luke. Approximately 6 billion people have now seen this film.

There is a scene in which Jesus delivers a person possessed by demons. Right at the exact moment in the film where Jesus commands the evil spirits to come out, one of the daughters, a girl of about fifteen, began shrieking and madly lashing out against everything and everyone around her. All hell quite literally broke loose among the hundred or so waiting patients. Our staff responded swiftly, and a team got the hysterical girl onto a trolley and into A & E. Her mother and sister, both quite distraught, followed alongside.

The girl was unresponsive, yet eerie sounds emanated from her mouth. Nurses had to restrain her in order to keep her from hurting herself. My wife immediately inserted a cannula and drew a blood sample for the usual lab tests. She then gave her 10 mg of Valium, the dosage that would normally bring an epileptic fit under control. It had no effect whatsoever on the girl. In the course of her thirty-year career, my wife has treated many children with seizures, but the raging creature before her was displaying symptoms unlike any she had ever seen before. She asked the mother a few questions about the girl's history, in the hope of gaining some insight.

The mother reported that her daughter had recently developed an interest in the occult. School students in

Europe are similarly attracted, and "play" with Ouija boards and related paraphernalia. Flirting with such dark mysteries gives them a bit of a thrill. But what starts as seemingly harmless fun can quickly turn into grave danger for some. Dressed in black, they begin to participate in satanic masses, worshipping evil incarnate. There are consequences. Their view of the world, their personality, and their behaviour all begin to change.

The mother reported that Nelida, her eldest daughter, had begun having these strange attacks three weeks earlier. They would begin whenever her younger daughter read aloud from her Bible. Nelida had been admitted to the municipal hospital in Abancay, where the doctors had pumped her full of four different psychotropic medications – to no effect. Perplexed, her doctors then referred her to a psychiatrist in Cusco with a provisional diagnosis of psychotic syndrome. They had also recommended a CT scan to rule out any organic reason, such as a brain tumour, for her bizarre behaviour.

Although Abancay is the capital of the Apurímac region, in 2012 there was neither a CT scanner nor a psychiatrist there. They had to go to Cusco. They were sent with a few forms, but were unaccompanied by a medical professional as they set out on the five-hour journey. On the Pan-American Highway, there is a large Diospi Suyana sign right at the exit for Curahuasi. As they approached, the mother suddenly asked the taxi driver to turn off towards the mission hospital.

The girl on the trolley remained unresponsive and continued to lash out. The look on her face was one of confusion. My wife decided to proceed with a CT scan. Five nurses helped her transfer the girl through the waiting area to radiology. One of the doors in the corridor got stuck. Agustin

Landeras, head of logistics, came by to help with the door. Martina asked him to call the hospital chaplain.

One minute later, they reached radiology. Two members of the department were waiting for them. Now there were ten people with this girl: my wife, a medical student, four nurses, radiology staff Alexandra Kopp and John Lentink, Agustin Landeras, and Pastor Santos. As they tried to contain the girl, a loud, ugly male voice suddenly came forth from the child: "I will not leave her. I will return!"

Everyone in the room began praying for the girl, praying out loud, each in their own language, all at the same time. They all believed this was a case of demon possession.

A horrible laugh came from the girl's mouth and the voice repeated, "I will not leave her. I will return!"

The staff responded, "You must leave her – in Jesus' name!"

Pastor Santos and Agustin held the girl's head in their hands. They later validated each other's report that the size of the girl's head kept changing. It was a surreal scene, straight out of a horror film.

After several failed attempts, they finally managed to get a scan of the girl's brain. It showed no anomalies.

They were all in the radiology department for about thirty minutes. The girl continued to rage with what appeared to be supernatural strength – ten members of staff struggled to hold her down. They wheeled her back into A & E, praying aloud continually. A paediatrician joined them and began to pray as well.

Again the horrible laugh and the voice declaring, "I am staying!"

Occasionally, the poor girl looked up and whimpered, "Help me, help me!"

Agustin Landeras left the room to call other staff for additional support. Within minutes, twenty-five Peruvians and missionaries had gathered in the chapel to pray continually for God's protection and intervention.

When Agustin returned to the girl's side, she turned to look at him with eyes as black as two deep, dark holes. Everyone heard the strange voice address Agustin directly: "You are afraid of me! Your heart is trembling!"

"Yes, I am afraid," Agustin responded. "But Jesus is more powerful than you are!"

The girl's face distorted grotesquely, and there was nothing human about the ghastly shrieking.

Finally, the voice spoke once more: "I am leaving, never to return!"

At that moment, the girl suddenly became quite still. When she came around, she was herself again. Pastor Santos prayed for God's protection over her. My wife began to ask her some basic questions, which she was able to answer coherently and in complete sentences.

However, she had no recollection of what had just happened.

If your worldview does not allow for the existence of evil spirits, then you must find an alternative, perhaps a medical, explanation for what happened in our hospital that day. Perhaps you would surmise that the girl had a severe personality disorder and this was an acute psychotic episode. Or perhaps it was an extremely unusual epileptic fit. For atheists, the existence of demon possession is out of the question; their attitude is that it should not exist and therefore does not exist. And yet the Bible illustrates a large number of scenarios involving demon possession, with the spirits being driven out in the powerful name of Jesus Christ.

By April 2019 our hospital had treated approximately 335,000 patients. Though the case above remains unique to our personal experience, it has much in common with multiple accounts both in the Bible and in Protestant and Catholic records throughout history. My wife and all the other eyewitnesses are absolutely convinced that this was a case of demon possession and deliverance. Everyone present describes a terrifying, other-worldly atmosphere, and they testify to the power of God, who intervened in response to their prayers.

But what became of the girl? In December 2014 I looked her up. Nelida was now enrolled in vocational training, and regularly attending church in Abancay. She was doing remarkably well.

The apostle Paul clearly spelled it out in his letter to the church at Ephesus: "For our struggle is not against flesh and blood, but against the rulers, against the powers, against the world rulers of this darkness, against the spiritual forces of evil in the heavens" (Ephesians 6:12, NET).

29

Front and Centre

You can be a master of rhetoric, able to speak for a solid hour without consulting your notes, but your discourse will only have impact if you make a personal connection with the audience – if you have them on the edge of their seats, so engaged they scarcely remember to breathe. To do that, you must be passionate about your material – that is the most important element of oratory.

The people in the auditorium are not stupid. They sense instinctively within minutes if a speaker truly has something of value to say, or if they are just filling time. If you are going to speak at all, do it with enthusiasm. You can only inspire others if you yourself are already inspired. Only what comes from the heart finds its way into another heart. Fortunately, my wife and I naturally reflect this zeal for Diospi Suyana; it is our whole life.

When Nelson Mandela was released from prison in 1994, the public held on to his every word. We were working in South Africa at the time, and therefore witnessed the incredible impact Mandela had on the entire population. The head of the African National Congress wasn't a bad speaker, but he had such extensive influence because he practised what he preached. He sacrificed twenty-seven years of his life, confined in prison, pursuing the idea of freedom. Nobody could have accused him of being all talk. Mandela's very life commanded respect, and this respect was thoroughly apparent on the faces of his audiences.

Are churches in Europe so empty because those up front no longer live their lives the way they encourage others to? Have they discredited not only themselves but also the Christian faith through blatant double standards? Is this why people are now almost ashamed to talk openly of God?

Since 2004 I have shared many a presentation – with Christians and atheists, academics and working class. I have had more than 2,600 opportunities in interviews and other appearances to share with my audience what is most deeply important to me.

When I first received the invitation to address the Young Nursing Professionals in Duisburg on 7 May 2013, I was very excited. But then the organizers let me know that I was to stay within neutral waters in terms of my beliefs. In other words, I was to be politically correct. Most people do not consider it appropriate for a guest speaker to use such a forum to share their personal convictions. In our postmodern society everyone is free to believe what they like – as long as they keep it to themselves. There is no tolerance for the assertion that one's view is the absolute truth, because people who think differently can become quite upset.

However, on the grand stage of public opinion, this call to neutrality is not universally applied or upheld. I recall once watching a TV talk show and hearing one of the guests tout the healing powers of stones. Others swore by the tenets of New Age cosmology or shamanism. All of these beliefs are tolerated, but that tolerance does not extend to Christian faith.

My concern was valid. If I edited out my faith in God from the story of Diospi Suyana, there would be almost nothing left. The name "Diospi Suyana" itself is a profession of faith, meaning "We trust in God" in the language of the Quechua. How on earth would I be able to speak about our work in Peru if I had to take out all references to faith?

As I made my way to the main entrance at St Mary's Gate on the morning of the event, laptop under my arm, I was met by Heike Viethen. She was a member of the organizing committee and had facilitated communication with the Young Nursing Professionals. In 2010 she had been considering coming to work as a nurse at the mission hospital, but then circumstances had taken her in a different direction.

Soon I was on stage alongside other invited speakers, familiarizing myself with the lectern. The technicians were sorting out the last glitches. For some unknown reason, the signal from my computer was not being picked up for projection onto the screen.

During these frantic eleventh-hour preparations, I looked out into the auditorium and saw the conference participants streaming in. Fifteen hundred nurses from all over Germany would soon fill the rows of seats, anticipating the official start. I had heard that the event was fully booked and that hundreds had been turned away. I began to feel very nervous. I am not usually one to suffer from stage fright, but this time was different. How would the organizers react if I started to share my beliefs?

The conference began. After the initial welcome, two professors each addressed the audience for thirty minutes. Then it was my turn. While I had been waiting, I had made my decision. I would give my usual presentation, unaltered and unfiltered.

I spoke quickly so that I could fit quite a comprehensive picture of Diospi Suyana into my allotted half-hour time slot. I was aware that my presentation would seem like fairy-tale nonsense to some people present. In the second half of my talk, I dived headlong into the taboo subject of faith, how it was the basis for our work and the hope that sustains us at Diospi Suyana.

Behind the curtain, Heike Viethen was becoming visibly uncomfortable. She too was fully aware of the constraints imposed by the organizing committee, knowing that it would have been much more acceptable to talk about any other subject than the one I had chosen – faith.

For a second, she considered coming to the podium, taking my microphone, and thanking me for my presentation, effectively cutting me off. Then she noticed the absolute stillness in the auditorium, so decided against that. The stillness erupted into a thunderous standing ovation after my last sentence.

In feedback provided to the conference organizers, my presentation about Diospi Suyana was the only one singled out by name in every response submitted. Without exception, everyone who gave feedback expressed the highest appreciation.

One participant wrote, "Maybe there really is something like a God who makes the impossible possible!"

Another comment from a nursing student in Cologne read, "Our respect goes to the work in Peru. Someone who has walked this path knows what it is like to trust in something you cannot see in order to accomplish something that will help others see."

Even one of the other speakers at the conference responded, "The hospital in Peru is actually something impossible, intangible. And yet there it is – right where no one would expect it to be!"

Pages upon pages of feedback made it clear that the story of Diospi Suyana had made an impression, eliciting goosebumps in many audience members as they listened.

I have often reflected on that May morning. Why did the audience jump to their feet and applaud the way they did? I think it was because I addressed the question at the heart of all humanity: is there hope after death? Almost nobody who has heard the long sequence of otherwise unexplainable providential events at Diospi Suyana has been able to remain indifferent. Sooner or later, a hope starts to grow inside – maybe the God of old really does exist, and therefore death does not have the last word.

Heike Viethen, a believer herself, wrote me a candid email after the conference: "I learned a lot from you on Tuesday. God really surprised me, because I was not expecting 1,500 people – Christians, Muslims, atheists, nuns – to stand up and applaud you the way they did. I have never experienced that in all the years I have been involved with this conference."

One day a woman said to me, "Dr John, God allows so many miracles to happen at Diospi Suyana because you won't keep quiet about them – you'll tell everybody!"

I find that an interesting thought. And yes, if that were actually the case, if our open acknowledgment of the Most High God were that important to Him, would He not create opportunities for us to shout His praises, with the biggest microphone? Some 2,000 years ago, Paul spoke at the Areopagus in Athens, the same location used by the council of city elders to debate the latest ideas. Towards the end of his life, he defended the Christian faith before emperor Nero in Rome. Do we have similar opportunities today?

It was a Saturday. I was sitting at my desk, perusing emails. One of them in particular grabbed my attention. The subject line read, "Dr Micha Bahr, Possibility of Joining Staff."

The unknown colleague was a consultant in paediatric surgery at the university clinic in Marburg. He had heard of me, read my book, and then come to the conclusion that we were actually related. His mother's maiden name was John. She had come from Silesia just like my late father. To eliminate any risk of confusion, my great-uncle Erich John stepped in and confirmed that we were in fact members of the same extended family.

In his detailed email, Dr Bahr expressed interest in the possibility of working with us in Peru. We receive emails like this every day. The dedicated staff at our office in Germany usually handle them. But his third paragraph really struck me. The president of the German Association of Paediatric Surgery had contacted him requesting a recommendation for a keynote speaker for the 4th World Congress of Paediatric Surgery. Dr Bahr had thought of me.

Two minutes later I had Dr Bahr on the phone. As relatives, we were immediately on a first-name basis, and he got straight to the point.

"Klaus," Micha entreated, "the World Congress of Paediatric Surgery takes place every three years in the capital city of the host country. In 2013 it is Germany's turn."

"Micha," I interrupted my second cousin, "that is all very well, but I am not a paediatric surgeon."

"That doesn't matter. The president of the German Association of Paediatric Surgery wants to show the human face of Germany. Not the impersonal precision of Mercedes-Benz or BMW, but the actual heart of Germany. You're the perfect man for the job!"

That phone call took place on 11 May 2011. Almost eighteen months later, I drove south to meet Professor Fuchs at the university clinic in Tübingen. I had four hours to think through my approach to this meeting. To be selected to deliver the keynote address at a medical World Congress is one of the highest honours a doctor could ever receive. I knew that. But what would the president of this German association make of Diospi Suyana? From almost all of my pictures, he would realize immediately that the story I had to share was one of faith.

I pondered the matter, praying aloud as I drove. Somewhere between Mannheim and Stuttgart, I knew what I had to do. Even at the risk of Professor Fuchs throwing me out on my ear, I was going to describe Diospi Suyana as I always do: as a work of faith.

At 1 p.m. a secretary invited me into the professor's office. Somewhat older than I, his slim build and angular face made a striking impression. He immediately introduced me to his colleague, Professor Seitz, who was also a member of the World Congress leadership team. He then encouraged me to open my laptop and begin my presentation.

Three-quarters of an hour later, the two professors looked over at each other.

"Dr John," Professor Fuchs said, deeply moved, "you're hired. You have twenty minutes for your presentation. Of course, it will need to be in English!"

On 13 October 2013, the walls of the plenary assembly hall were bathed in dark blue light. Three years after the 3rd

World Congress on Paediatric Surgery had been held in New Delhi, Professor Fuchs opened the 4th World Congress in the Berliner Congress Centre. The Dresden Boys' Choir sang their first piece, then a dignified Professor Aziskhan stepped up to the microphone. The president of the World Federation of Associations of Paediatric Surgeons (WOFAPS) shared the right words for the moment.

More songs and speeches followed until the words "Special Lecture" with my name underneath appeared on the screen. It was time to hear the baker's boy from Wiesbaden, who had found his destiny in the Andes mountains of Peru. Once again, I shared the story of Diospi Suyana, this time with surgeons from all over the world.

My twenty minutes were sufficient to share 120 photos of Diospi Suyana history. At the conclusion of my presentation, I took my leave with the following words: "This evening, Hindus, Muslims and Christians, agnostics and atheists have gathered in this congress centre. While I respect your beliefs and convictions, if you were to ask me what explanation I would personally give for the incredible development of Diospi Suyana, I would tell you that I am convinced it was God. He caused it to be built. It was the power of Jesus Christ!"

GOD HAS SEEN US

30

Off to Great Britain

Diospi Suyana began as just a small seed of an idea in Tina's and my heart, but over time it has grown and become widely known throughout the world. How is that? Certainly not because of the millions of dollars we have received in financial gifts. Any medium-sized company moves considerably greater sums than that, and nobody thinks anything of it. With a current staff of 260, including our missionaries, Diospi Suyana would be considered one of the smaller organizations on the market. So why all the fuss about it?

The exciting thing about Diospi Suyana is not what we have done, but what God has created. All of this has been His divine providence. His miracles have aroused a high degree of unanticipated attention from Christians and non-Christians alike. Those otherwise inexplicable "coincidences" and answered prayers are enough to give pause to consider the possibility that God is more than a figment of an extremely dogmatic and delusional imagination. Christians, regardless of their denomination, have been so inspired by the Diospi Suyana story, they have become personally involved and shared their enthusiasm with those around them.

In September 2014, I made my first trip to Great Britain for the purpose of sharing my presentation. At the end of the 1980s, my wife and I had worked in England and Wales for a couple of years, but we had lost touch with almost all of our acquaintances over the twenty-three years since then. Nevertheless, this tour from Cardiff to Newcastle, London to Birmingham, was not only made possible, but actually turned out to be a great success, largely due to a man named Adrian Gibson.

In August and September 2014, Adrian Gibson was most often found at his desk, phone in hand. In fact, he made more than 500 calls to painstakingly arrange my schedule in Great Britain. In addition, he sent more than 500 emails to companies, churches, journalists, and private individuals. As a top executive at Hilzinger, a tool company in Tuttlingen, he surely had other demands on his time. Why did he invest so much effort in Diospi Suyana?

We often compartmentalize the people we meet in life, usually unaware that we are doing so. But to what kind of "box" could one possibly commit Adrian Gibson? There is nothing ordinary about this white African from Zambia. Zambia, Zimbabwe, South Africa, Germany: all the countries he has lived in and the backdrop of an extraordinary life.

In 1992, Adrian married Cordula Hilzinger and became part of a successful family business. Soon he was travelling all over the world, networking for the company. Highly ambitious, he enjoyed his work very much. Adrian sought success and found it. A pretty wife, two healthy children, and a stimulating job – it was the life many can only wish for.

During the afternoon of 23 March 2011, Adrian was out jogging through the fields of Tuttlingen. At forty-eight years old, he was healthy and physically fit. When he returned home from his run, he still had energy for some additional exercise in the spare room. Out of the blue, he felt a shock run through him from head to toe. Thinking he had possibly pulled a muscle, he decided to take an aspirin and lie down.

That evening, Cordula noticed that something wasn't right. She phoned the doctor, who had him admitted to Tuttlingen hospital immediately. In the middle of the night he was transferred by ambulance, lights flashing and sirens wailing, to the Neurosurgical Intensive Care Unit in Schwenningen. A CT scan revealed a subarachnoid haemorrhage.

The successful businessman lay helpless in Neuro-ICU, hooked up to monitors that reported the blunt truth of his physical condition without regard for anyone's feelings. Sluggish from medication, Adrian sensed that he was at death's door. When Cordula called the ICU for an update later that evening, she received the devastating news that her husband might not survive.

Cordula wanted to drive to the hospital the next morning with their sons, Victor and Felix, and her brother Holger. They might be compelled to say goodbye to their beloved husband, father, and brother-in-law.

It was 26 March 2011 – Adrian's forty-ninth birthday. He remained in the Neuro-ICU, fighting for his life, fading in and out of consciousness. He began to hallucinate, and in the middle of all the cacophony, he kept hearing the same question, over and over: "Where do I go from here?"

Adrian prayed. He tried to negotiate with God, even though he wasn't 100 per cent sure He existed. He began to realize that he could have all the success in the world but still not be fully alive. He suddenly knew deep within that he would survive. God had work to do through him!

Adrian did recover. At the beginning of 2012, he was driving from Tuttlingen to Stuttgart, when on impulse he pulled over into a parking area. He took out a copy of *I Have Seen God*, given to him by friends the previous Christmas. The hours flew by as he read, recognizing himself in the story: the longing for God, finding meaning and fulfilment in Him alone.

On 18 May 2012, the Tuttlingen city hall was packed. Several companies had shared the cost of hiring the location. City mayor Herr Kamm was deliberating on dreams that come true. At Adrian Gibson's invitation, I shared the story of our hospital in Peru. The hall, at capacity with its 288 seats filled, became still and a bit tense, as men and women representing all elements of the local community realized that the doctor from South America was talking to them about God, and about a deep hope that there is more to life than just our few years here on earth.

When the Tuttlingen event had concluded, Adrian Gibson voiced a novel idea: "Klaus, the story of Diospi Suyana needs to go to England. We need the book in English and you need to go to that country."

Following my tour of England, I still had a few things to take care of in Germany before returning to Peru. I was suddenly presented with an amazing opportunity to share the Diospi Suyana story even further with the British – this time long distance.

It was a Friday evening, 26 September 2014. I was sitting in the Southwest Broadcasting (SWR) radio studio in Germany, where a recording with BBC 5 was scheduled for 9:30 p.m. Several technicians were working to improve the sound quality on the telephone line. Of course, it was Adrian Gibson again who had been responsible for making a host of phone calls and setting up that evening's opportunity.

"Is that Dr John?" Stephen Nolan, the popular radio presenter, asked.

For almost half an hour he asked me about Diospi Suyana and my faith in God.

"Many of us just stumble through life without any sense of meaning or purpose," Nolan said towards the end of our conversation. "But with you that is obviously not the case." Stephen Nolan, the man who had won the Sony Gold Award seven times and had even been voted Britain's best radio presenter in 2003, was discussing the meaning of life.

"That's true," I said, after a short pause. "What I have always really wanted to do is watch God at work."

This radio interview was broadcast in its entirety throughout Great Britain on 8 November. So far, six English magazines and newspapers have featured articles on Diospi Suyana. Whether via Christian or secular media, hundreds of thousands of British people have been presented with the message of faith. Adrian Gibson made it all possible. In ICU, battling death, he had sworn, "I want to use the time I have left to serve God with my talents."

And he kept his word.

31

Around the Globe

Travelling can be fun. My most precious childhood memories are of holidays with my family. My father would close up the bakery and my mother would let the blinds down in the shop. In the window there would be a big sign declaring: CLOSED FOR HOLIDAYS. A few days later, my parents would cram several suitcases and four kids into our estate car, and at the crack of dawn we would head off to our holiday destination.

Travelling alone, however, is not so much fun. At least, I don't care for it. But in order to spread the word about Diospi Suyana, I have accepted it as a necessity. I know how lonely a hotel room can be. I know how frustrating searching for parking in an unfamiliar city can be. I know the feeling of panic when your flight is suddenly hit by turbulence. And I am no stranger to the delays and tailbacks on European and American motorways. I often watch the clock and worry about reaching my destination on time. When I finally return to my hotel room late each evening, I am usually greeted by close to fifty emails, some of which require an immediate response.

As good residents of the German state of Hesse, my wife and I gave our first presentation in the local Rhine-Main area back in 2004. This was followed by a number of opportunities all across Germany, then invitations to Austria and Switzerland.

Since we opened the Diospi Suyana hospital, my wife has stayed on site in Curahuasi to lead the team there. And so we have different roles: my wife works and I talk. I made a very smart move when I married Tina in 1987. Without her management expertise, I would not be able to be away from the hospital for long periods of time. But it has worked out quite well. My presentations have inspired those in the audience, building up a wide circle of support for Diospi Suyana, and attracting numerous highly skilled volunteers. That said, I really don't consider myself a "storyteller" – I just relay the facts, which clearly speak for themselves. One presentation might open the door to the next. I have met the most interesting people along the way, some of whom would make brilliant characters in a book!

On 29 October 2008 I met one such person following a presentation – a young man of about twenty-five who approached me in the cafeteria at Kulmbach Hospital.

"Can I come and work with you?" he asked directly, with a beaming smile.

"May I ask who you are and where you are from?"

"My name is Anti Pertula and I am a medical student from Finland. I am currently studying in Munich for a semester."

"Where did you hear about us?" I enquired with growing curiosity.

"In August 2007 I was on the train from Vienna to Bratislava. There was a copy of the German Rail magazine, *DB Mobil*, in my compartment. It contained an article about you and your wife. I took a look at your website a few months ago and noted the dates of your presentations in Germany, and I took the train from Munich to Kulmbach."

"That's a three-hour trip!" I exclaimed.

"A little longer," the man admitted. "I had to change trains twice."

"What is it about Diospi Suyana that interests you so much?"

He responded, "I read on your website that you are less interested in theological hair-splitting and more concerned with putting your faith into action. That clinched it for me."

At 10:30 that night, we were both on the motorway heading towards Munich. I drove the young man home, then planned to continue on to Salzburg. We had a three-hour opportunity to continue our dialogue.

"There is an association of Christian doctors in Finland," Anti told me. "You really must share your presentation with them!"

As we parted ways at 1:30 a.m., he promised me, "I am coming to Curahuasi, you can be sure of that. I will see you first in Helsinki, then Peru!"

I headed back towards the motorway in the drizzling rain, dreaming of the enchanting Finnish lakes.

Two years later, I was finally in Helsinki, speaking to a crowd of 200 mostly young people at a church in Suhe. My translator was none other than the young medical student Anti Pertula. He had kept the first part of his promise and met me in Helsinki. Now we just needed to get him to Peru!

In February 2013 I spoke in several German communities in the sweltering Chaco province of Paraguay. On a clear, starry night, more than 100 young people listened to my speech out in the open air, crickets chirping in the background. And in November of the same year, I spoke in Manitoba, Canada, where the temperature was an icy -20°C.

A Catholic doctor organized an opportunity for me to give my presentation in northern Italy, and a medical student sent me to her church at Garstang in Lancashire, England. A reader from Mexico invited me to his country, and a Spanish lady arranged for me to go to Barcelona to give a series of presentations after she had devoured the Spanish version of my book during a transatlantic flight.

Every time I share the story of Diospi Suyana, I strive to tell it as I did the very first time, full of passion and honesty. The post we receive often tells of astounding changes in the lives of those who have heard it. At the Catholic Petrinum-Gymnasium in Brilon, Germany, 350 pupils listened intently, mesmerized. Their religious education teacher started praying and reading the Bible again after hearing the story.

Shortly before Christmas 2007 I had the opportunity to speak to 500 students at an independent Christian school in Lörrach. I asked Frau Rabus, the teacher who had coordinated the event, how much time I had to speak.

"Knowing my kids, I'd say ten minutes. After that they will have stopped listening!" came the refreshingly direct reply.

As it turned out, Frau Rabus was mistaken. The children sat silently, completely engrossed. You really could have heard a pin drop.

It was six years before we received any feedback from Frau Rabus. Then the following letter arrived at our German office:

> It was awesome when Dr John came to our school
> a few years ago! I will never forget his presentation,
> and I can still picture the students and staff, jaws
> dropped, as they listened to the Diospi Suyana story.

It was the highlight of all the worship services we had ever held up to that point. I will never forget those pictures or the miracles that God did, and the enthusiasm with which Dr John shared his story. I remember thinking that he didn't even stop to catch his breath – surely, he would collapse soon! None of us really dared breathe either – we were just so captivated by what we were hearing.

I too was in awe. Two people had had a vision, and God used them to build something completely magnificent. When people ask, "What difference could I possibly make?" it is often more of an excuse than an actual question – and it is completely absurd.

Included in the letter with Frau Rabus's kind comments was another invitation to speak. Of course, I would not turn that down. So on 6 April 2014, I again shared the story of Diospi Suyana at her school. This time, I had to do the presentation twice, as the fire code dictated that the crowd of 600 students be split. I addressed the younger and the older students in separate services.

One student, known for generally detesting such school assemblies, told his teacher afterwards, "That was the coolest thing I've ever heard!"

Throughout my travels I make every effort to say what I think, and to live out what I say. When Jesus charged His followers to "pick up their cross", He meant that we should be willing to sacrifice, even suffer, for His cause. The integrity of a Christian is not determined by what he or she says, but by living a life that is consistent with those words and pleasing to God. I would like to share a personal example. Since the

GOD HAS SEEN US

beginning of my presentation tours, I have never once turned on a TV in a hotel room if I am alone. I want to be faithful to my wife, and the content of many modern TV shows – even those not considered "pornographic" – can lead our thoughts in directions I'd rather mine not go. Christian leaders are not immune to the charms of money, sex, and power. To be sure, those temptations have led to the downfall of many.

32

To Have or not to Have: $25,000

During the month of November 2014, I drove more than 8,000 miles through twenty-five US states to give fifty-eight presentations, nearly half of which were for radio or TV. My thoughts were of course often with my family and Diospi Suyana back in Peru.

I knew there were some problems there. Two of our claims for VAT reimbursement, totalling $25,000, had still not been processed by the Peruvian tax authorities, SUNAT, and we had no idea whether or not they would agree to pay. Our bookkeeper had not been able to submit the claims during the authorized time window because we had been waiting for a required document from the Agencía Peruana de Cooperacíon Internacional (APCI). The APCI regulates the activities of all large NGOs operating in Peru. Three months passed before the APCI sent us the document we needed. Too late, unfortunately, as the window was closed. Everyone seems to acknowledge and even expect bureaucratic inefficiency, but I was unsure if the tax office would be sympathetic to our plight. I may have been on the road far away in North America, but in my heart I was in Peru, the middle of the mess – and praying for a solution.

I arrived home on 2 December, and immediately phoned our bookkeeper.

"Señor Montalvo, how is it going with our claims? I need to know what is going on!" I demanded impatiently.

"Dr John, don't worry. One of the clerks told me it was all proceeding, but I can enquire at the tax office in Cusco," he attempted to reassure me.

Unfortunately, verbal promises in Peru are about as reliable as a weather forecast for next month. I didn't let it go. "I need something in writing!"

On 4 December, Ivoska Seiffert visited my office. Frau Seiffert is none other than the sister of the former president of Peru. She has lived in Switzerland for many years, and it was her daughter Carol who had volunteered with us for two months as a dentist, following a recommendation from the president himself. Now she was here to pick up her daughter. We offered her a private presentation and tour of the hospital.

"Frau Seiffert, we might need your help," I said at the end of my presentation. "I will soon be hearing whether or not the tax office has agreed to reimburse the VAT we paid in January and February. It is a significant amount of money."

"Dr John, I would be happy to help you if it is needed. I will be visiting my family in Lima before returning to Switzerland."

The very next day, and to my bookkeeper's great surprise, the very thing I had dreaded came to pass. The tax office denied our claim. Within seconds I had my phone in my hand – $25,000 is a lot of money for a mission hospital to lose – and was placing a call to the president's sister. It was a Friday. The weekend passed. On Monday, we were back in contact. Ivoska Seiffert had told her brother and his wife of our difficulties. When they understood that Diospi Suyana was in danger of losing $25,000 because of the inertia of a government agency, they promised to rectify the situation.

"Dr John," Frau Seiffert assured me, "if you send an email to this address today with all the documentation attached, the First Lady Nadine Heredia will attend to it first thing tomorrow morning."

I almost always believe in striking while the iron is hot. We needed to hurry. Agustin Landeras, head of our logistics department, drove with me that night through the mountains to meet up with Edgar Montalvo and compile all the necessary information. Owing to the dense fog, it was midnight before we reached his office. At the same time, our head of administration, Marion Hofmann, ploughed through the hospital archives, searching for any pertinent records.

By 1:30 a.m. I had all the paperwork in hand. At 3 a.m. Agustin and I were back at my desk in Curahuasi, composing a letter to the president and his wife. At 4 a.m., in the cold light of dawn, I pressed "Send", then went to bed, and Agustin headed home.

Perhaps you are familiar with that "unsettled" feeling, when there is a lot at stake and you just can't get your mind to let it go. So you toss and turn, as sleep remains elusive. By 5 a.m. I was back at my desk, preparing a presentation, because later that very day, APCI was coming to inspect all the hospital equipment that had been donated.

After the chapel service, I invited the APCI visitors from Lima into my office.

"It is a great honour for me to be able to share the story of our work with you," I said kindly. "Afterwards, you can begin your inspection tour."

The officials, a smartly dressed woman and a well-mannered gentleman, graciously enjoyed the cake and tea that my secretary, Gabi Wall, had provided for them. Soon they were sitting up straight in their chairs, absorbed in my presentation.

As part of the presentation, I shared how over the years various authorities had blocked our path and made things difficult for Diospi Suyana. I said that now the same thing was being done by their own agency, the APCI.

"Dr John, *mea culpa* – my fault," confessed Jessica Flores, one of the APCI representatives. "APCI has been without a director for the last several months, so many things have gone off course."

Two days later, the APCI representatives headed back to Lima. What they had seen first-hand at the hospital and school had certainly made an impression. My focus admittedly had been less on our guests and more on the situation with the tax office. I checked my emails every hour and phoned the president's office several times, but with the World Climate Summit taking place in Lima the following week, everyone there was frantically busy. I had fallen off the radar and was beginning to lose my patience.

Then came the call that finally put us out of our misery. On Wednesday 17 December, Señora Juscamaita, the president's personal assistant, phoned me.

"Dr John, I have just got off the line with the general director of the tax office in Cusco. She is aware that the president is personally concerned with this matter. You have an appointment with her on Friday. Let me know how it goes."

Early Friday morning, 19 December, following a wonderful staff Christmas celebration the evening before, I drove down to Cusco. I met our bookkeeper at the entrance to the tax office at 8 a.m. A few minutes later, we were ushered into the director's office. Two clerks were also present.

"Dr John," Director Martha Velarde began, "everything is OK. We have accepted your VAT claim. The refund cheque should be with you in a few days. Please sign to indicate your acknowledgment on the back of this form."

I had a solemn look on my face, but inside I was grinning. This was so typical of Peru: a government error had cost us $25,000, but a word from the president turned the whole situation around.

The very week we had received the depressing news from the tax office, the president's own sister was in our hospital, wandering the corridors in amazement at all she saw. Another strange coincidence? But why? I believe it is because our life assignment is God's business. When we are working for Him, He will not let us down. Furthermore, He hears and responds to prayers. Throughout all of history, He has done so. The prayers don't need to be eloquent or grammatically correct; they need only come from the heart.

One of the prayers that has most moved me was heard during my US tour. I had just wrapped up a presentation in front of 230 students at the Houston Presbyterian School, and the children were about to return to their classes.

A teacher hurried to the front and said, "What we have just witnessed is a miracle – let us pray!"

Everyone present listened attentively, but no words came. The teacher was weeping. She closed with an "amen", and her prayer was finished.

33

Please, Come into Our Bedroom

Perhaps you think God only intervenes in major affairs and matters of high public interest, such as Diospi Suyana. The reporters are there, the cameras, and perhaps the president himself will just drop in via the hospital helipad.

But is God also willing to act in our individual lives, yours and mine, when nobody is looking? That's what this chapter is about. I would like to invite you into our bedroom in Wiesbaden.

We live in Peru, but since I am in Germany so often, travelling around and presenting, we also have a small flat in the attic of my sister's house. Our bedroom in this flat is tiny, only about 7 m². As with many attic rooms, the space is further confined by a sloping roof. We managed to squeeze a double bed into this space when we were on furlough in 2011. Between the bed and the fitted wardrobe, there is a space of 45 cm. We wanted to put a chest of drawers in front of our bed, next to the door. But while the pitch of the eaves gives a cosy and safe feeling I quite enjoy, it is extremely difficult to find furniture that fits into a space like this. If you're not sure what I mean, check out the photo section in this book. If the chest of drawers were a bit taller, then it couldn't be as wide, or it simply wouldn't fit under the eaves.

We went around all the furniture stores in the Rhine-Main area, as we needed wardrobes and desks for our three children. We found just about everything we wanted – except for a chest of drawers for our bedroom. The sloping roof was one problem. In addition, our bed was made of beech. It had been on special offer and my wife hadn't been able to resist the ridiculously low price. So our chest of drawers needed not only to fit; it also had to match.

Perhaps you are thinking that this really shouldn't matter to a missionary family. Perhaps we should just be content with a bare cell in a monastery… Regardless, one afternoon I set out on my own, determined to find a suitable chest of drawers before sunset. I wanted a quality piece of furniture, made of solid wood, exactly the right size, in a beech finish, at a price that wouldn't bankrupt us.

I marched doggedly through the furniture stores, praying as I took the escalators up and down. Not arrow prayers, more like a constant plea: "Please, God, help me to get this chest of drawers matter settled!"

I am sure you can identify with the motivation for my efforts on behalf of Diospi Suyana. We save so many people's lives and the mission hospital has truly become a beacon of hope for the whole region. But why would I be similarly driven just for a chest of drawers? You'll have to excuse me, but once I get something in my head I have to see it through.

I hurried through the first furniture store, then the second, and still a third. At Dänisches Bettenlager (a Danish furniture shop known as JYSK in the UK), I saw a small chest of drawers made of pine. It was beautiful, but the yellowish tint would clash with the beech bed. One could argue that it doesn't really matter since our eyes would be closed at night anyway. I suppose I am a bit strange – nobody knows that better than my wife.

Over the course of three hours, I looked through five furniture stores, beseeching the Almighty for a bonanza. Doesn't God have more important things to worry about than this mere trifle? We could probably argue that for hours. But Jesus did encourage us to turn to Him in prayer, even for the little things, as trusting and naïve as a child. I have spent part of my career at Harvard and Yale, and I still most assuredly believe this to be true.

The afternoon had flown by. It was now evening and I still hadn't found a chest of drawers. Finally, I popped into the XXXL furniture store in the Äppelallee-Center in Wiesbaden. No luck. I stood at the exit and looked at my watch. It was twenty minutes to seven, I noted grumpily. I was out of time, and now I was compelled to ponder all the theological reasons as to why God might have chosen to ignore my three-hour spiritual plea.

Just to the left of the Äppelallee was a Real supermarket. While it seemed like clutching at straws, I decided to have a look. Perhaps God would answer my prayer in this unlikely place.

A Real store is the German equivalent of an ASDA or a Walmart. There is a large food section, some inexpensive clothing, basic housewares and office supplies, etc. A Real would not be the first place you would look if seeking furniture, but at this point I was desperate.

I asked a cashier if they stocked any furniture.

The lady was busy ringing up a customer's purchases, but responded briefly, "I don't know. If we do, it will be on the next floor." She pointed towards the escalator.

You can probably imagine how I was feeling as I stepped onto the escalator. I had combed through six large furniture stores in search of a chest of drawers and come up empty. Now I was in Real, just a few minutes before closing time. It was the end of the line.

I walked up and down the aisles, but couldn't see a single piece of furniture – not a bed, a cupboard, a table. Nothing.

Then I spied some cardboard boxes towards the back of the store. They had the sort of labels you might expect on boxes containing pieces of furniture. As I got closer, I could see that one label was printed with a picture of a chest of drawers – very much like the pine one I had been admiring at the Danish Bedroom Store. I picked up the box and immediately ripped it open. I couldn't believe my eyes. The chest was made of pine, but it had been stained. It would be a perfect match for our bed. At €99, this was the least expensive chest of drawers I had encountered all day.

As I dragged the box to the till and paid with my card, I started to have doubts. Perhaps God really had heard my mumbling all afternoon, and this was an answer to prayer…but what if the chest didn't fit under the eaves? There are moments, though, when we feel a push from God, much like a tailwind. This was one of those moments. If you are not a Christian, this might sound strange, but never mind – keep reading.

I proudly carried my purchase up to the third floor and began assembling the many parts. The stained pine next to the beech of the bed was quite aesthetically pleasing, if I do say so myself. I regarded the finished product before me, then slowly eased it back, under the eaves. What I saw completely overwhelmed me – the drawers fit as perfectly as if they had been custom made for the space.

The next day, I showed my sister Helga this crowning achievement.

"An atheist would never imagine that God would answer such a prayer!" I said.

My sister aptly replied, "Neither would most Christians."

Ouch.

In churches all over the world, prayers are said every Sunday beseeching God to ease the pain of those who are suffering and to comfort those who are hurting. Most of the prayers are fairly generic and the answers are not easily verified. I can understand why 96 per cent of Germans prefer to stay in bed on Sunday mornings. Such prayers seem complete hogwash to them, perhaps an exercise in futility. Why get up for that? But when we pray very specifically, down to the minutest detail, it can be quite thrilling to see how God responds!

When I am travelling around Europe, I occasionally stay overnight in Wiesbaden and catch a few hours of sleep in that double bed under the eaves. Actually, it is much too big for me without my wife. But when I open my eyes in the morning, I see the chest of drawers whose size and colour remind me of the goodness of God. I drive off to my next presentation, knowing that God is my Father in heaven who delighted to grant me my heart's desire for a chest of drawers.

My earthly father used to always tell me, "Klaus, we have to pray about the little things too!"

How did he know? I'll tell you in the next chapter....

GOD HAS SEEN US

34

Back to the Future

As dusk fell, only dim outlines of rough shapes were visible in our living room. My three siblings and I were mesmerized as we listened to Papa tell us the story of his escape. My sisters Gerlinde and Helga, my brother Hartmut, and I had heard the story often enough. In fact, we knew every detail of those harrowing two weeks when my father, a prisoner of war, escaped from France and made his way back to Germany. He sought cover in the forests along the way, continually afraid he would be recaptured or even killed.

It is 19 August 1947. My father throws himself into a thicket. A French border guard spots him. The guard's dog rushes to where my father lies trembling on the ground, obscured by the dense shrubs.

My father tries to hold his breath, crying out to God in his heart, "God, save me! I want to go home to my parents who are sick, and to my brother Walter."

The French guard grows impatient and swears coarsely. What is wrong with this dog? It is specially trained for sniffing out prisoners, and yet it is running back and forth as though it has lost the scent.

Nearly a week later, on 25 August, my father is somewhere on the Germany–Luxembourg border. *It's all over now*, he thinks. A Luxembourg guard has suddenly appeared from the north. My father is hiding behind a tree, too petrified to move a muscle. The soldier strolls up and down the border, his eyes focused on the other side. Just one glance to the left, and he will discover a fugitive in tattered clothing just a few yards away. My father sends up one arrow prayer after another.

The next day, my father has crossed over the border into Germany. He is exhausted and penniless. Who will help him, a man on the run? Then he spots an old man who has been a customer at his father's bakery in Silesia.

"I know you!" the man, who is himself displaced, calls out. "Come with me – you can sleep at my house and I have a little bread for you."

On 29 August, my father is on his way to the train station. Suddenly, a car pulls up beside him.

"Where are you heading?" the stranger behind the wheel asks.

"To the station," my father replies.

"Then jump in!"

A few minutes later, the kind stranger drops my father off at his destination. As they say their goodbyes, the man pushes a 20 Deutsche Mark note into his hand. My father realizes at this point that he doesn't have any money with which to buy a train ticket. At the ticket office, he pays 19 Deutsche Mark for the journey to Bad Schwalbach in Hesse.

The John family saga stretches way back. At least five generations have lived in faithfulness to God, and have been held in high regard in their Silesian community in Güttmanndorf near Reichenbach.

Once, the village policeman knocked at my great-grandfather's door and informed him he had been accused of a significant wrongdoing.

The baker protested, "Officer, you have known me for years. I am a God-fearing man!"

His word was enough to convince the officer. "Yes, this is true. I will drop the charges."

The decision as to whether or not to trust in God must be consciously made by each individual, but in some families, including the Johns, there is a vast wealth of experience and numerous examples of lives lived in faith. As this is passed down from one generation to the next, the younger cannot help but be influenced by those before them, and they are encouraged to trust God with their own lives as well.

I will admit that our family life is a bit different from the "norm". For one thing, I am away from my wife for six months of every year. In total, I have spent more than seven years apart from Martina. She leads the team in Curahuasi while I am on the road. How she manages to fulfil her roles as a committed doctor, co-leader of a mission, and mother, I will never know. Actually, I do – God has given her a rare combination of talents. She is absolutely dedicated to her work and family, and demonstrates an abundance of expertise, intuition, empathy, and love.

"Where will the Johns be in ten years' time?" I am often asked during my presentations.

If God continues to bless us with good health and strength, we would like to keep on until we retire. We constantly have new ideas for Diospi Suyana. We would like to increase the inpatient treatment capacity. Numbers in themselves are not the goal – we recognize that every patient is a person, and we want to help as many people as possible. We see the long queues at our entrance each morning. We see the people camping outside in the hope of getting an appointment. My wife and I are deeply troubled by this and we're all the more determined to help as many as possible while we are alive and able to do so.

We have started Radio Diospi Suyana and in the future we would like to flood the whole of southern Peru with broadcasts on health, culture, and faith. We are currently looking for volunteers to commit to this project on a long-term basis.

Although we were the ones to initiate the work, Diospi Suyana does not depend on us. God can replace us at any given moment, should we need to step back because of ill health. That day will come – one day. Olaf Böttger, Chair of Diospi Suyana Germany, and his sister Annette, who heads our foundation, are also committed to Diospi Suyana for life and would no doubt step up. Dr Jens Hassfeld would make a competent leader of the multiple aspects of the Diospi Suyana ministry. He may well do an even better job than we do.

What are our children up to? After graduating from high school, our daughter volunteered for a year at an orphanage in South Africa. As this book was going to press, both Natalie and Dominik were pursuing medical studies in Germany. It must be hereditary. Florian also lives in Germany. After attending high school in the USA for a year he is continuing his education in Wiesbaden.

When my wife and I pop home for a quick lunch, we often see pupils in the Diospi Suyana school uniform pass by. I can still remember my own route to school. The bell used to ring at 1:15 p.m., proclaiming our freedom until the next day. My friends and I would jump up and race through the door. Six school periods are simply exhausting. On my way home, I used to dream of what I might be later on. Perhaps an explorer, a researcher, or even a missionary doctor. Of course, I had no concrete ideas about my future back then, but it seemed that all options were open to me.

I often speak to people about their own stories. More often than not, they describe their childhood as somewhat idyllic, and they gaze back with a touch of romantic nostalgia. But beyond childhood, life gets tougher, and people characterize more-recent days in less pleasant terms. At the thirty-year school reunion, they are confronted with the realities of heart failure, early onset disease, and even death. Most of us don't really have any interest in going back in time. Back to school? No, thank you! Apply to university again and pull all-nighters in preparation for exams? I'd rather not. Get up repeatedly in the middle of the night to pace the halls attempting to soothe a colicky baby? I am very glad those days are over.

We move forwards and our thoughts are of the future, even though we know that our journey will inevitably conclude with the grave. Then what? One might say a life is merely an unavoidable dead end. If that were all there was to life, it would leave a nasty taste in my mouth and a big question mark in my mind.

The Bible speaks of our life on this earth as a time of preparation. The best is yet to come. That is what Jesus promised us. That is why we are Christians.

Sometimes people tell me that they are quite satisfied with the here and now. That when the lid is lowered on their coffin, then that is it – and it's enough. I don't believe them for a second. The seed of eternity is planted in us – the Bible tells us so. Literature and music are full of longing for the hereafter. The musical *Cats* in particular enjoyed great success not just for its dazzling musical composition but also surely for its theme of eternal life.

35

Finally, and Most Importantly

Many years ago, way back in high school, I met a young woman. Everyone who knew her spoke highly of her. She was decent, kind, and helpful. Her nature made her very popular with fellow students. She didn't do drugs, sleep around, or shoplift. Her strong sense of order and her diligence, along with her superior intellect, indicated a promising future ahead. She came from a respectable family. She was confirmed at the age of fifteen and accompanied her parents to church every Christmas. If there were an award for being a "good Christian", she would have stood every chance of earning the title.

When she was sixteen she had a riding accident. She fell off her horse, then the horse fell on top of her. Suffering from a complicated pelvic fracture, she was confined to the hospital for five long weeks. This gave her plenty of time to think. She realized that she could have been killed in the accident. In the quiet and solitude of the hospital, questions nagged at her – Does my life have a purpose? What happens when we die? – but she had no answers.

A few months after being discharged from the hospital, she came into contact with a Christian youth group where these very questions were being discussed – and answered. She was amazed to hear that God lived, not at some great distance, but here with us and in us. She heard how Jesus Christ

GOD HAS SEEN US

sought to make Himself personally known to every single individual. That empty space so many try unsuccessfully to fill with money, success, sex, etc. – she was learning that it was meant for God alone.

Two years later, this young woman made a conscious decision. She entrusted herself – her past, present, and future – into the hands of God. From this point on, she wanted to live her life in fellowship with Jesus Christ. Following this decision, she was filled with a joy she had never known before. Her most secret sins, nailed to the cross of Christ, were gone forever. She sensed Jesus' closeness in a very real way. Whatever trials she might have to endure in the future, she knew she could never fall further than the loving hands of God.

Perhaps you have figured out who this young woman is. Yes, she is indeed my wife. We have been married for more than thirty years.

My own childhood was markedly different. For my parents, their faith was the absolute foundation for everything they did, including how they used their money. They lived out a solid, authentic faith before us. But faith cannot be inherited from a previous generation. Each person must experience it and live it out for themselves.

Interestingly, I too went through a period of searching, much like Martina did. As a medical student, I had seen many people die. I was no stranger to the fear of death. Like others, I went through the "Medical Student Syndrome" in which I would often perceive myself to be experiencing the symptoms of a disease I was studying. Just a mark on my skin and I would be panicking about malignant melanoma. A sore knee and I was worried about bone cancer.

One time, I was standing at the bedside of an alcoholic. All of a sudden, several varicose veins burst in his oesophagus. He bled to death within minutes, right before my eyes. His last words are indelibly etched in my memory: "What will become of me?"

That dying patient asked the very question I had been asking: what will become of me when I draw my last breath, when they carry my body to the grave? I just had to find out whether the hope spoken of in the Bible was wishful thinking or something much more.

One cold November evening, I was crossing a large field. The wind was howling and leaves were swirling through the air. The outward conditions mirrored the state of my soul. I was so restless and agitated.

I gave vent to my feelings and bellowed into the darkness as loudly as I could, "God, where are You? I want to see You!"

Maybe you will agree with me that in the story of Diospi Suyana, God has become visible. I am convinced of it. That is precisely why I chose the title *I Have Seen God* for my first book.

And because God sees all of us, including you, I want to encourage you to give faith in God a try. You have nothing to lose and everything to gain. I am sure that God can fill that empty space in your heart too, just as He has done in mine and Tina's.